THE NEW PUPPY OWNER'S MANUAL

Some other titles from How To Books

Protecting Your Identity
*A practical guide to preventing identity theft and its
damaging consequences*

Seven Ways for Anyone to Boost their Income
*How making a few simple changes can significantly reduce
your outgoings and gain extra income*

Spending the Kid's Inheritance
How to ensure you have the time of your life in retirement

Your Own Allotment
How to find and manage one – and enjoy growing your own food

Free Yourself From Anxiety
A self-help guide to overcoming anxiety disorders

Send for a free copy of the latest catalogue to:

How To Books
Spring Hill House, Spring Hill Road
Begbroke, Oxford OX5 1RX, United Kingdom
info@howtobooks.co.uk
www.howtobooks.co.uk

THE
NEW PUPPY
OWNER'S MANUAL

'A great investment for all excited or anxious owners of a puppy!'

ANGELA FITCH

howtobooks

Published by How To Books Ltd
Spring Hill House, Spring Hill Road
Begbroke, Oxford OX5 1RX, United Kingdom
Tel: (01865) 375794, Fax: (01865) 370162
into@howtobooks.co.uk
www.howtobooks.co.uk

How To Books greatly reduce the carbon footprint of their
books by sourcing their typesetting and printing in the UK.

British Library Cataloguing in Publication Data
A catalogue record for this book is available from the British Library

ISBN 978 1 84528 287 5

Illustrations by Phillip Burrows

Cover design by Baseline Arts Ltd, Oxford
Produced for How To Books by Deer Park Productions, Tavistock
Typeset by Kestrel Data, Exeter, Devon
Printed and bound by Cromwell Press Ltd, Trowbridge, Wiltshire

NOTE: The material contained in this book is set out in good faith for
general guidance and no liability can be accepted for loss or expense
incurred as a result of relying in particular circumstances on statements
made in the book. Laws and regulations are complex and liable to change,
and readers should check the current position with the relevant authorities
before making personal arrangements.

Contents

Introduction

This book is written especially for all puppy owners looking for help with puppy behaviour, training and general advice. It is not designed to be a technical guide, or to offer histories and facts that, while very interesting, won't help you at home, today, with training your puppy.

I have tried to cover all the questions that puppy owners have ever asked me. You will find the chapters very comprehensive, written in a step-by-step format and with solutions following problems that you may experience in each area. The first section concentrates on puppy behaviour, as well as advice on grooming, health and feeding related topics. The second section focuses on training, that is, giving you practical exercises so that you can begin training your puppy.

There are a couple of important things I want to mention here: Firstly, remember that dogs are pack animals and, as such, they need a leader. This *has* to be you, and the section on pack hierarchy applies to *you*, whether you own a Yorkshire Terrier or a Rottweiler.

Secondly, when training, re-read the training guide at the beginning of the chapter before you begin any new exercises. Unless you follow the training guide, you will not achieve the results you are looking for. I always practise these principles when training, so study them, because when *you* learn to reinforce them, you will see that communicating with a dog becomes an awful lot easier.

Finally, I have referred to your puppy as 'him' throughout this book. Please don't be offended if you have a 'her' – it was only to make the text uniform and so that the writing would flow. Happy Puppy Days!

Part 1

The Basics

1

Bringing Your New Puppy Home

BEFORE YOUR PUPPY ARRIVES

It is very exciting when you bring your new puppy home. Puppies are great time wasters, keeping the whole family from doing all they should, while you all watch them play, eat and even sleep. They are wonderful fun for all the family, and friends. However, the better prepared you are for your new arrival, the more enjoyable he will be to have around. I have visited many families who are struggling to cope with the demands a new puppy can make. Owners can be completely unprepared and unaware of just how having a puppy in the house will affect their everyday lives.

This chapter is designed to give you advice on the essential and not so essential (but can't help yourself) equipment and accessories you will need to consider buying. You will also find other advice concerning bringing a puppy into the home which I am sure you will find useful.

By now, you will probably have chosen your puppy and have hopefully researched your chosen breed carefully. Many problems arise simply because owners choose a breed of dog that is just not suitable for their personality or lifestyle.

Puppies are not robots so we cannot make them behave as such, and nor would we want to. However, being prepared for the needs of your puppy before he arrives should help you enjoy these early months, rather than finding yourself becoming frustrated and angry because he has slowly but surely started to take over your days – and nights.

THE FIRST DAY

When you bring your new puppy into your house, remember that he may feel disorientated and possibly stressed at being removed from his old home, his mother and his littermates.

Give him time to settle in and if you have a young family, remind them to give him some space and not to keep crowding him or be constantly picking him up. Puppies do often settle in really quickly, so help him to do so by being prepared for his arrival.

Young puppies will sleep regularly. They need to, so remind all family members that if he has gone to sleep, they should leave him alone for a while. This is a good rule to enforce with children

- Puppy pads or newspaper

- Scent removing cleaners

- Water bowl

- Food bowl

- Puppy collar and lead set

- Toys of different textures: i.e. soft, hard rubber, rope

- Small puppy training treats

Dog crate

I cannot tell you how many times I have heard 'I don't want to put him in a cage'. I do understand peoples concerns and worries over doing the right thing, but I am here to tell you that getting a crate (I know it looks like a cage) is definitely one of the best investments you can make for your puppy. It will speed up the housetraining process, it will keep your puppy and your furniture safe while you are out and it will give him a cosy, safe den to sleep in. There are no negatives here. I do not know of any vet, breeder or trainer that doesn't recommend using a crate. That surely must tell you how great they are.

Introducing a crate

1. Find a quiet corner/area to put the crate.

2. Put your puppy's soft bed at one end and leave space for a puppy pad or newspaper at the other end (for night-time or when you go out).

3. Introduce your puppy to the crate by putting his toys in there. You can feed him some meals in there and play with him in

there (sticking your arms in of course, because I doubt you'll fit). You could also try leaving a few treats for him to find in there, when he wanders in of his own accord.

4. Leave the door open until your puppy has made a positive association with the crate.

5. He will start to run in and out of the crate on his own, and he will probably settle easily to sleep in there without prompting. Don't provide any other bed in other areas. Not doing so will help encourage him to settle into his bed in the crate more quickly.

6. Begin closing the door without any fuss. Just close it, turn and walk away – you should find that your puppy will be happy to stay in there.

TIP: CRATES

Buy a crate big enough for your puppy to stand up, turn around and stretch out – remember he will grow. However, if your crate is *too* big, as your puppy gets older, he may get into the habit of toileting at the other end rather than beginning to 'hold on' for longer periods of time.

The maximum amount of time to leave a puppy in a crate is up to four hours (unless at night-time). When you start leaving your puppy during the day, you need to gradually build up to this time. Don't just shut him in his crate and go out. Get him used to being in there while you are in and around the house.

Dog bed

There are plenty of beds to choose from. My advice is to get one which can easily be washed as accidents can and do often happen. You will need to regularly wash the bed anyway so either choose one with a removable cover or a fleece-type bed which can just be picked up and put in the wash.

Puppy pads

Puppy pads are mats which are treated to attract your puppy to toilet on them. I am not a lover of using them although they do serve a purpose in the early days. The reason I am not so keen is because, in my experience, owners can rely on them too much, encouraging their puppy to use them indoors and then having trouble with training their puppies to toilet outside. Use the pads or newspaper to leave down for your puppy only at night-time, or in the early days when you go out. (See Chapter 2 on housetraining for more detailed information on this subject.)

Cleaning liquids

It is essential that you use proper cleaning products designed for the job of cleaning up those little accidents. Do not use your normal household cleaners: invest in a product which will be effective at completely removing the smell of urine and faeces.

Water bowl and food bowl

These are self-explanatory really but try to get a heavy water bowl as puppies will often have a great game with a bowl of water, tipping it all over the floor. You will probably need a small, low-sided bowl to start with, which you can change to a bigger one later if necessary. I would avoid using the dual water/food bowls as you may find your puppy (and floor) can get really messy, while he is thoroughly enjoying tucking into his food and splashing water all over the place.

Puppy collar and lead set

This may not be essential straightaway but it won't hurt to be prepared. Although your puppy won't be walking outside yet, you may like to use it when you visit the vet and frankly, the sooner you introduce the collar and lead, the sooner your puppy will get used to it. Don't leave it until you want to take your puppy out for a walk. He will have enough to cope with just being introduced to the big wide world. Purchase a soft weave set to start. They are often easily adjustable and lightweight, to help your puppy get used to the feel of having a collar around his neck. Section 2 on training has advice on introducing a collar and lead to your puppy.

Toys

There are hundreds of toys on the market. Try to purchase a good variety of textures, shapes and sizes which your puppy will find rewarding to chew on while teething. Try to include tough rubber toys, plush toys, rope toys and those which have various textures all on the one toy. Cheaper toys may be easily destroyed and potentially dangerous to a puppy who likes to eat what he has 'killed', so choose carefully. Remember to supervise your puppy with those toys which could cause him to choke. If you rotate the toys he has access to, it will keep him more interested in them when you bring them out to play, as opposed to leaving them available, all of the time.

Treats

Treats are a great reward for a puppy and you will use them when you start housetraining and practising the basics as you work through Section 2 on training. Make sure you purchase treats suitable for your puppy's age and don't use any which are highly coloured as they are laden with artificial colourings.

HEALTHCARE

The Vet

You will need to consider a few points when choosing a vet to use for your puppy. You should think about their location, their opening hours and whether they provide a 24-hour service in case of emergency. You may like to visit a surgery to see how you feel about it and, if possible, actually meet with the vet. You can ask other owners or friends which vet they use and whether they are happy with them. Personal recommendations are often a good starting point. You need to find out the costs for vaccinations and other services which may be relevant for you.

Questions to ask your vet:

1. What are their opening hours and 'out of hours' services?

2. How much is a general consultation and how much are the vaccinations you need for your puppy now?

3. What is the timescale for getting vaccinations done and when will your puppy be able to go out?

4. If you have specific ideas about caring for your dog, check that the vet has these too, i.e., do you want your dog castrated? Is your vet happy to provide this service as

routine or will they only do so for medical or behaviour recommendations?

Vaccinations

Most owners will bring their new puppy home when they are eight weeks old. Vaccinations are required to protect your puppy against a variety of diseases including the following:

♦ Distemper

♦ Hepatitis

♦ Parvovirus

♦ Parainfluenza

♦ Leptospirosis.

Normally, a puppy will require two visits to a vet for vaccinations. Often, the first will be at eight weeks and then two weeks later you will return for the second vaccination. It will be up to two weeks after this time that your puppy can safely leave your home.

You can see that administering vaccinations is a four-week procedure so, whatever age you start, you are generally looking at four weeks before your puppy should go out. Remember that most vets will recommend an annual booster of these injections and this normally only requires one visit. Check when this will be due and the cost involved.

Parasites

I feel I should include some information of worms and fleas. I don't want to blind you with science but you may find a few basics of interest so you know what to look out for. I have listed a few of the more common parasites but, as with anything, prevention is better than cure. Speak to your vet about the regular treatments they have available and remember to regularly give your dog's bed and living areas a good clean. I hope you don't encounter many of these.

Roundworms

Mothers often pass these onto puppies before they are born. They can also be caught by puppies suckling on their infected mothers skin or from ingesting eggs in soil. These worms resemble strands of spaghetti. These worms can be passed onto humans.

Treatment

Mothers will be routinely wormed. Puppies are wormed before they are two weeks old and regularly thereafter (in accordance with veterinary advice).

Tapeworms

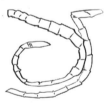

These, the most common worms, are caught by eating an infected flea. They can also be caught from uncooked meats. The eggs are passed in the dog's faeces, and when dry they resemble grains of rice. Some may occasionally be seen moving around the fur near your dog's anus. Some dogs may experience itching in this area. These worms can be passed onto humans.

Treatment

Worm in accordance with the vet's advice. Avoid uncooked meats, fish and game.

Whipworms

These eggs can live for years in the environment and dogs can ingest them by accidentally eating them, causing them to grow into adult worms. They are thicker at one end, hence the name. They can cause acute diarrhoea and stools are often bloody with mucus. A severe infestation can cause the dog to lose weight and suffer abdominal pain.

Treatment

Worm in accordance with the vet's advice. Keep the environment clean and disinfect regularly to get rid of the eggs.

Hookworms

These are small thin worms. Puppies can acquire them via their mother's milk and often adults become infected by larvae penetrating through their skin. They cause bloody/black diarrhoea, weight loss and weakness. Eggs appear in the faeces two to three weeks after exposure.

Treatment

Worm in accordance with the vet's advice and thoroughly clean the environment.

Fleas

The larvae of fleas are activated by heat. People often notice fleas during warmer weather although they are now an all-year-round problem due to central heating. The larvae evolve into fleas which then look for blood that they feed on. They hop onto your dog and can hop off again. They feast by biting through the skin and cause itching and redness in most cases. You can see their 'dirt', tiny black specks, on the skin.

Treatment   *Treat according to the vet's instructions, usually flea treatments. You also need to treat your house regularly as fleas/larvae may be living around the home and garden.*

Ticks   These are usually picked up in long grass. The tick attaches to your passing dog and sinks its mouth into the skin. It sucks as much blood as possible until it bloats into a tiny white balloon. It then drops off.

Treatment   *You can remove ticks but you must be very careful not to leave the head in your dog's body while pulling it out as the tick may survive or you may risk infection. There are 'tick removing' grooming tools available to help with this.*

Ear Mites   These are often caught from another dog and puppies can catch them from their mother. They are often irritating at night and cause wax, dirt and itchy ears.

Treatment   *Treat according to the vet's recommendation.*

Scabies (Sarcopin mites)   This is often caught from dogs or foxes which already have scabies. It is extremely itchy and mainly affects the tips of the ears and elbows.

Treatment   *Treat according to the vet's recommendation.*

Cheyletiella mites	Mostly seen in puppies, these are caught from their mother. They cause a thick dandruff over the dog's back but it is not always itchy.
Treatment	*Treat according to the vet's recommendation, usually anti-flea treatments.*
Lice	These are often found in dirty and unhygienic environments. The lice leave eggs, called nits, attached to the dog's hair. The lice make dogs itchy and if a dog is really infested it can cause blood loss and anaemia.
Treatment	*Lice can be eradicated with good flea treatments. Use according to the vet's recommendations.*

GROOMING AND HANDLING

Bathing

It may be tempting to give your puppy a good wash every week. I am well aware of all the muck they love to roll in. However, you really shouldn't bath a dog more frequently than every six weeks. Too much bathing can ruin their coat by upsetting the natural balance of oils. If necessary, rinse areas with water in between 'proper' washes and a thorough regular brushing will also help to keep him clean.

1. Be prepared – get the bath ready and have towels to hand. I normally use a shower attachment, it is less messy and I can thoroughly rinse the soap out of the coat.

2. Put a nylon collar on your puppy – this is to 'hold on to' in case he decides to make a dash for it. Use a lead if necessary.

3. You can insert cotton wool balls into his ears (not too far) to stop large quantities of water running inside.

4. Get rid of any knots in his coat first – when they get wet, the knots will tighten even more and be more difficult to remove.

5. Be safe – use a non-slip mat to avoid your puppy slipping.

6. Use a proper puppy/dog shampoo – I often use a 'no more tears' baby shampoo around the head and face. Remember to rinse all shampoo out completely to avoid irritating your puppy's skin.

7. A dog will normally shake when their head/ears get wet. Try doing the body, feet and tail first to save yourself getting a good soaking right at the beginning.

8. Don't let your puppy outside in the cold weather if they are still wet – towelling well and using a hairdryer can speed up the drying process.

Teeth Cleaning

You can train your puppy to accept you brushing their teeth. I would start from about four to five months old. Brushing regularly will help keep his teeth and gums healthy. You can use a finger toothbrush or a dog toothbrush (similar to the ones we use). Make sure you buy a dog toothpaste. Using a nice meaty beef or chicken flavour will certainly help you to keep him interested. Your puppy will swallow toothpaste so it is important for this reason too.

1. Be prepared – Have the brush ready with the toothpaste on it.

2. Gently but firmly, raise his upper lip and gently brush the teeth and gums.

3. If he is calm, you can offer a treat and praise.

Keep these sessions short and successful. Gradually increase the brushing and areas you cover each day. Do not chase your puppy and pin him down, it will either become a game or you will terrify him. Tempt him with the treats and stay relaxed yourself.

Your puppy's gums should be pink and look healthy. Any sign of inflammation or bad breath may indicate a problem and you should check with your vet.

Ear Cleaning

Never stick anything right into your puppy's ears. A little wax is normal and ears can be easily cleaned using an ear cleaner from the vet or pet shop. Gently wipe the visible inside of the ear, using cotton wool. Some breeds (i.e. Poodles), as they grow older, will also have excess ear hair. This needs to be regularly removed. Ask your vet or groomer to show you how. A sign of possible ear problems is your puppy shaking his head and scratching at his ears. Often the first sign of infection will be a bad smell. Have a sniff every now and then to check them out.

Eyes

Your puppy's eyes should be bright and clear. If they are red or teary, ask your vet to check them for you. Infected eyes often produce a yellowish discharge. Some dogs will regularly have a secretion from their eyes, it is normal and helps keep their eyes clean. If your puppy is a breed which is prone to 'sleep' around their eyes, make sure you clean the area daily to avoid it building up into an uncomfortable and irritable problem.

Brushing/Combing

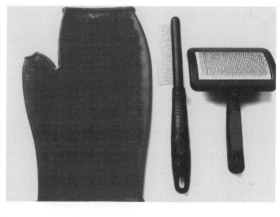

There are many grooming products on the market and you need to purchase one which will do a good job for your breed. If the brush is too soft, it will simply glide over the top coat, leaving everything underneath untouched. If it is too harsh for a silky or short haired breed, it may well be uncomfortable and scratch their skin. If in doubt, ask your groomer but I would generally go with the following.

♦ Long or thick coat breeds – Slicker brush followed by a comb through.

♦ Silky coat breeds – soft slicker brush followed by a comb through.

♦ Smooth/short coat breeds – Hound glove.

1. Be prepared – have your brushes, combs and treats within easy reach.

2. Use a lead to stop your puppy running off around the house or garden – it also helps to influence calm behaviour.

3. If possible, raise your puppy onto a table with a non-slip surface – you can buy rubber mats/bath mats if necessary. You will find grooming much easier if you raise him up like this.

4. Never allow your puppy to play with a brush – if he thinks it is a toy he will keep playing with it. If he tries to bite it, pull it away while saying firmly 'no'. If your puppy is highly focused on playing with your brush, offer a treat to distract him. Hold onto the treat for a few seconds while he licks it, before you actually let him eat it. During this time, brush him and praise him for standing still. Gradually build up this positive

association with being brushed until your puppy readily accepts that he is not to bite the brush.

Although shorter haired breeds will not get matted, regular brushing will help remove loose and dead hair, helping to keep his coat and skin healthy.

Grooming is a simple and effective activity for asserting your authority over your dog, so not only will it keep his skin and coat in good condition but also it will help reinforce your leadership.

Nail Trimming

Dogs will need their nails trimmed roughly every six weeks if they have not worn down naturally. If your dog walks regularly on concrete, you may find that his nails get filed down anyway due to the surface he is walking on. Others will need to get their nails trimmed with clippers. Nail clippers come in small or large sizes so choose one suitable for the size of your dog. The guillotine style of clipper is the most popular.

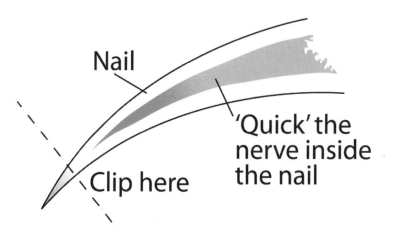

A dog's nail has nerves running through the centre, known as the 'quick'. If you cut the nail too short, you risk cutting these nerves and causing them to bleed. This, of course will hurt your dog and he won't be very accommodating when you try to do it next time. If the nails are white, you can often see the quick but if they are black, you need to judge where to trim. You can ask your vet or groomer to show you how to trim your dog's nails, as investing in nail clippers yourself will save you time and money over the years to come. You can buy a blood coagulation powder from pet shops if you do have any accidents by trimming a nail too short.

TIP
If you trim your puppy's nails regularly from a young age, it will prevent the quick from growing very long inside. This is how you can keep your dog's nails reasonably short throughout their life.

Handling
Remember to practise handling your puppy every day. Be confident and persevere to achieve what you are trying to do. If your puppy tries to back away or tries to bite your hands away, then you need to work on practising handling those areas. If you back off in response to this behaviour, you are teaching your puppy that he can be successful in stopping you by behaving this way. If you continue to allow him to 'see you off', over the long term this will make the problem harder to cure.

From a young age, running your hands along your puppy's body and legs, as well as doing health checks such as looking at and touching around his eyes, ears, tail and paws, will help ensure that he is happy to accept you handling him all over.

Practising handling is a worthwhile exercise. If your puppy is injured and in pain, you will have more success in helping if he trusts you to handle him. Dogs which haven't been taught to accept this, can often become snappy or aggressive when owners or vets try to touch them, commonly disliking them touching their feet or tail end.

FEEDING

There are many varieties of food on the market. The first choice for you is whether to feed dry or wet foods. Personally I only use dry, I find it more convenient. Either way, the food you choose should be nutritionally adequate for your puppy. With regards to ingredients, there will always be a label but owners often find them difficult to understand. In view of the fact, this book is not designed as a technical guide, I will not go into too much detail regarding analysis of ingredients. I will mention just one ingredient however – protein.

Protein

This is what most owners look for when buying food. We know that protein does a great job within the body, including tissue repair and blood clotting as well as assisting with your dog's immune system. It also can be converted and stored as fat. There are many dogs whose behaviour has been dramatically improved by changing their diets and reducing the amount of protein they have. For all these reasons, owners may try to choose the lowest protein containing food – but here comes the important technical stuff.

Calculating protein levels

In order to check a food's protein levels to compare them to others, you need to do some calculating. Simply reading the label will not give you an accurate comparison. In order to get the true amount of protein within the actual food, you need to convert what it says on the label into a dry-matter basis. Basically, this means getting the protein content of the actual food after all the water has been removed.

Calculating protein content
Look at the guaranteed analysis of your food and then:

1.   100 – percentage of moisture = A
2.   Percentage of protein ÷ A = Percentage of protein on a dry-matter basis.

Different protein requirements

You can obtain this information from food manufacturers directly, but I think it is important to point out that reading the label on this matter is not as straightforward as I know many owners think it is. Dogs require different levels of protein according to their age and activity levels. In the following box is a general idea of protein requirements for different types of dogs.

Minimum guidelines for protein intake

Type of dog	% Protein required
Puppy/growing dog	22%
Adult dog	18%
Lactating bitch	28%
Working/highly active dog	25%

Dry Food

This is a very popular food nowadays. Basically, the ingredients are cooked under pressure and then dried. Fat is then added to make the food more appetising and then a preservative is added to avoid this going 'off'.

Dry foods are very convenient to feed as they can also be used as rewards in training and in various activities to provide stimulation for your dog.

TIP
Remember that when feeding 'complete' food it expands within the stomach. Always read the manufacturer's guidelines for the correct quantity to feed your puppy. If in doubt, speak to your vet for advice. Some owners will think that a portion of dried food may 'not look enough', but I can assure you that it is more filling than it looks.

Put some food in a bowl and add water to see for yourself what happens.

As a general guideline, you can use the puppy variety of these foods up until about six months of age. From there, you can switch to a junior/performance complete food which will also provide all the essential nutrients and calories your growing puppy will require. Then, when your puppy reaches the age of one, you can switch to the adult variety. Again, you should read the manufacturer's guidelines of your chosen brand. There are also other varieties available, including those for senior dogs as they get older or lower calorie foods for those who are overweight. Choose the most suitable food for your dog *and* lifestyle.

Wet Food

These are tinned meat and are referred to as wet food. Some are nutritionally adequate on their own but others will require a 'mixer'. This means you need to add biscuits to it to provide the other nutrients that your dog will need. This food is vacuum packed and so does not contain preservatives, although this means it will spoil within 30 minutes of being opened (sometimes sooner, particularly if it is hot).

My problem with wet food is that it restricts your feeding methods and it doesn't help to clean your puppy's teeth and gums, which the texture of the dry food will do. If you use wet food, remember to provide good chew toys for this purpose and get into the habit of regularly brushing his teeth.

Undoubtedly, the majority of dogs find wet food more appetising but most will happily eat dried. I know many owners who feed dried food as their main food but add just a little wet to make the food more appealing. In our house, we sometimes include a little

fresh meat or vegetables to offer a meal with different textures
and flavours. This works well by making a meal more interesting
and keeps a dog guessing about what he'll be getting. However,
beware of doing this every day or providing too much of the
'little' extras, because you can tip the balance and end up with a
very fussy eater.

Treats

There are many, many dog treats on the market now. Please
read the ingredients before you buy and if there isn't a list of
ingredients, then don't buy it at all. Don't be fooled by the
packaging: many of these treats come in stylish, attractive
packaging which can often tempt you to buy them.

Some treats are highly coloured so you can immediately tell that
there are colourings in there. Try and stay clear of these. Lots of
treats are cereal based or can be very fatty. Watch out for high
protein levels which with some dogs, if fed too often can cause
over-active behaviour. My advice is, as a general rule, steer clear
of most mass-produced treats. This sounds a little harsh and of
course the odd one or two probably won't do any harm, but there
are far healthier and tastier options for you to use. I have met
owners who have store cupboards dedicated to holding all their
dog's treats and some who feed so many of these during the day,
that their dogs won't eat their dinner in the evening. I know also
that often owners think they are doing the right thing, and that
these chews and treats are essential for their dogs because some
are even marketed this way. They are not essentials, so try to
think of them as sweets, and ask yourself how many sweets or
bars of chocolate your puppy is having each day.

Treats for training

I only use treats for training purposes. If you stop feeding treats for no reason, your dog will work harder for them when you need them to help you train. Try sticking with fresh meat. Chicken, beef and liver are very popular and if your dog likes vegetables, some consider carrot and apple (no seeds) a real treat. You can also buy training treats – small meaty rewards with no artificial colourings – which are also very popular. When training, you need the treats to be small and quick to eat. Using big munchy, crunchy biscuits may be just as enjoyable but by the time your dog has stopped to crunch it up and then licked up all the crumbs, he will probably have forgotten what he got it for in the first place.

> **TIP**
> While your puppy is very young (8 to 16 weeks), use the training treats which are available for young dogs, and if using fresh meat, chicken is the best option for now until they can cope with digesting richer meats.

To give your dog a more satisfying 'chew', then you can offer rawhide chews but I don't recommend you give them to young puppies. As they get older, you may introduce these and also look for other natural foods like pigs ears which most dogs really enjoy.

Feeding Times

When you collect your new puppy, your breeder will hopefully give you a feeding routine to follow. They will advise you what food your puppy is eating already and at what times. Of course, it is up to you if you keep with their choice or choose your own. Either way, I would keep on their original food until they are well settled in with you and if you decide to change brands at anytime, then remember to gradually introduce the new food over a period of one to two weeks. Simply mix a little of the new with the old, increasing the quantity of the new while decreasing the old, during this changeover period. This should help you to avoid any upset tummies.

As a general rule with feeding, most puppies from eight weeks of age will be eating three to four meals a day. This will continue until three to four months when you can reduce to just three and from five to six months you can reduce to two meals a day.

Suggested feeding times
1st meal 8am
2nd meal 12pm
3rd meal 5pm
4th meal 9pm

When you reduce to three meals, cut out the 9pm feed first.

When you reduce to two meals, cut out the lunchtime one.

Foods to avoid

As your puppy gets older you may be tempted to give him human food or treats. Watch out for foods that will be harmful to him. Here is an important list of foods you should avoid.

Chocolate

Plain chocolate or others with a high content of cocoa solids are particularly risky, but milk chocolate is also dangerous. There are chemicals in chocolate which can kill dogs, so don't be tempted to feed this to your dog – even a small amount can be lethal.

Bones

Bones can splinter and the worst culprits are chicken and turkey. (Incidentally, turkey skin is also to be avoided, vets have reported that it can cause pancreatitis). I would also avoid lamb bones as these too can cause problems. Even when cooked, these types of bones are dangerous and can do a lot of damage to your dog's internal organs, that is, if they haven't choked on them first.

Fruit

Grapes, raisins and apple seeds are all toxic and owners should be aware that these are not suitable treats for any dog. In fact, there are a number of stones and seeds which can cause problems for your puppy so to be on the safe side, I would advise that you avoid him having the opportunity to eat any stones, pips or fruit seeds at all. Apples without the seeds are perfectly good however. Vegetables are a healthy option as well. Try raw carrot for example. Many dogs enjoy the 'crunch' which comes with eating raw vegetables.

Onions

Watch out for onion in any leftovers you are thinking of giving your dog. It is not advisable for dogs to eat onions as they can lead to anaemia caused by damaging their red blood cells.

Nuts

Walnuts and macadamia nuts should be avoided.

Poisonous Plants

As well as some foods being dangerous for dogs to eat, some plants are too. A puppy does not automatically know which ones are 'bad' for them as I know some owners assume. You should check out your garden as young puppies in particular can be prone to eating all sorts of things they come across when unsupervised!

The list here is not exclusive but includes the following

- Crocus
- Clematis
- Daffodil
- Geranium
- Ivy
- Lilies
- Mistletoe
- Morning Glory
- Poinsettia
- Rhododendron.

If you have a garden with a variety of plants, you should check whether you have any which are likely to cause a problem for your puppy. Your vet should have a list of every single 'poisonous plant' in addition to those common ones detailed here. Generally, as dogs grow older, they will stop eating things like plants anyway.

Eating Poo

While on the subject of eating, dogs do sometimes eat unsavoury items and their own poo is actually quite a common favourite.

Coprophagia is a very common occurrence among puppies and many owners express concern about this. If your puppy is healthy and up-to-date with worming and vaccinations, then this activity shouldn't cause them any actual harm. It just isn't very pleasant, and you should try to avoid them doing this where possible. The best method is to interrupt your puppy and distract him onto something else, such as a toy. You should try to get his attention before he starts eating and always clean up any poo, rather than leaving it in the garden to be 'found' later. You will be pleased to learn that for puppies, this behaviour is very common and most of them grow out of it, particularly when you start doing more with them, such as walking and training.

Neutering

There are those who say you should and those who say you shouldn't! My opinion is that if you are keeping your dog as a pet you should get him neutered. This will only serve to improve your puppy's well-being, helping to avoid infections and diseases such as cancer and urine infections.

If you do not neuter, you will always be competing against hormones, finding it harder to train your puppy as he grows older. Males often become highly focused on scents from local females in season and both sexes are prone to scent marking around your home as well as proving harder to live with, aggression being a common complaint.

I find dogs tend to be happier around each other when they are neutered, with the competitive and challenging hormones out of the way, they are more relaxed and often able to get along better. Many vets neuter at 6 months old, you should plan for this whatever sex your dog is.

2

Housetraining

THE RIGHT WAY TO DO IT

Housetraining your puppy is all about communication. You need
to successfully communicate to your puppy that he needs to go
outside to the toilet. Once you have done this, he will understand
what it is you want, and most dogs are happy to do it for you.

The procedure is quite simple, and there are only a few things
you actually need to do. However, you need to do these things
well, and be consistent if you want your puppy to understand your
message.

Timing is critical. You only have one second to praise or correct
your puppy for going to the toilet. If you are too late – forget it.

Reward is essential. You need to make it worthwhile for your puppy to go outside to the toilet, otherwise, why would he bother?

Puppies are normally capable of being housetrained by the age of six months. However, many are 'clean' before this age. It is not uncommon for them to be eight or nine months old before lasting through the night. Using a crate for your puppy generally helps to speed up the housetraining process.

If you want to wait until your puppy has had all injections before letting him into your garden, then you will need to use paper or puppy training pads. Place one by the back door only and one in his crate at night or when you go out, until he is ready to go outside. Do not lay pads or paper around your house.

Either way, when you are going to let him outside, this is what you do.

Before you start
1. Do not leave any paper or puppy training pads on the floor for him to toilet on during the day when you are in.

2. Have a pot of small, quick to eat, flavoursome treats by the back door.

3. Buy a reputable cleaner specifically designed for cleaning up dog urine and faeces. There are a few on the market but you are looking for a good quality product to destroy the bacteria and completely remove the scent. Whichever you choose, generally, the rule is, the more expensive the better.

When you are ready

1. Restrict your puppy's access in the house. You cannot teach him to 'go' outside if he is messing in the lounge while you are in the kitchen. Use child/dog gates to help you keep his freedom restricted, then, when he needs to go to the toilet, you will see and be able to correct him.

2. Take your puppy outside at key times when he may need to relieve himself. These are after waking, playing and feeding. For a young puppy (8 to 12 weeks) you should take him outside every hour. If he is a little older, you may be able to leave it a little longer.

3. You must go outside with him. Wait for five minutes. If he does not go, you can come back inside. If however, you are sure he may need to toilet, remember to restrict his access so you can catch him in the act if he starts to do it indoors.

When he goes to the toilet outside

1. When you go outside, pick up your treat pot and take it with you.

2. While he is actually relieving himself, tell him he is a 'good boy'. You can also put a cue word to it, i.e. 'good boy to toilet'. This way he will associate a word for going to the toilet and in future when you are going out or going to bed, he will understand your request to relieve himself beforehand. Remember your timing. You use the praise and the cue word *while* he is doing it.

3. The second he has finished, before he has a chance to get distracted, offer him a treat, which you will have ready in your hand.

When he goes to the toilet indoors

1. If you find a mess or a puddle that he has done while you were out or not looking, then simply clean it up. Do not scold or punish your puppy. Remember the one second rule.

2. If you see him about to wee or he is already doing it, interrupt him, perhaps by jumping up, clapping your hands and calling his name. This should make him jump and stop him in the act.

3. Run to the back door, calling for him to follow you. You can bend down and open your arms to make him want to run to you if he is hesitating. Do not use a stern or cross voice.

4. Do not use the word 'no'.

5. When he reaches you, encourage him outside, wait for five minutes, during which time he should want to start where he left off. Use the praise and reward as detailed previously.

It is unlikely that you will stop your puppy while pooing. However, most puppies learn to poo outside more quickly than they do to wee. This is achieved by getting him outside at the right time by looking for signals that he is about to poo, such as sniffing the floor and circling on the spot.

WHAT HAPPENS IF YOU DO IT THE WRONG WAY

These are some ways that puppy owners train their dogs that can lead to problems.

Miscommunicating

Remember that dogs learn by association. They will make a link between an event and the result which follows it. Many dogs get confused because their owners don't communicate with them effectively.

If you tell your puppy off for messing in the house, you run the risk of your puppy thinking you are telling him off for going to the toilet, not for going to the toilet in the house. There is a big difference.

This in turn, may lead to your puppy thinking you will get angry when he goes to the toilet and may run off and do it in odd places when you are not looking. Or he may try to get rid of the evidence by eating it. Some puppies will develop urine infections because they 'hold on' because they know you don't like it if they do a wee. These are the reasons we never tell them off and if you communicate effectively, then you shouldn't feel the need to tell them off.

Not cleaning up properly

Toileting is a scenting activity for a dog. Haven't we all seen dogs thoroughly enjoying having a good sniff where the rest of us fear to tread? It's an important point, that if you do not clean up the mess properly with an effective cleaner, he may well pick up the scent of where he has been before. When he is learning to go to the garden to toilet, if he picks up a scent of where he has been before, he may forget about getting to the garden, as the smell can act as a trigger for him to go indoors again.

Overusing puppy pads

If you leave puppy pads all around your house, you are encouraging him to go to the toilet in all those areas. Dogs are very habit forming, and when you want to remove the pads or newspaper, your puppy may not even notice whether it is a puppy pad or Axminster carpet under his feet.

Too much freedom

If you give your puppy too much freedom around the house, you will probably miss any signs that he needs the toilet and you won't be able to catch him in the act if he starts to go indoors. The more success you have at rewarding your puppy outside, the quicker he will become housetrained.

Not going outside

If you don't go outside with your puppy, you will not be in a position to praise and reward him. You will miss your one second timeslot and no amount of yelling 'good boy' through the wind and rain or rattling treat tins from the back door will provide the effective feedback that is required.

Carrying your puppy

While your new puppy may enjoy being regally carried to 'do his business', if you scoop up your puppy and carry him to the back door, he will not learn to think about the route he needs to take when he needs to get there himself.

COMMON PROBLEMS AND SOLUTIONS TO HOUSETRAINING

These statements below are common problems that people encounter when housetraining their puppies. My solutions follow.

My puppy keeps toileting in the same area indoors again and again

♦ Make sure you are cleaning up with a proper cleaning liquid from the pet shop.

♦ Try and break the habit by obstructing that area so he cannot get there.

♦ Try feeding him in that area for a while.

My puppy won't go in the garden but when I bring him back indoors he relieves himself straight away

♦ He may not be comfortable toileting on a different surface. Try taking him to a different area, i.e. grass or concrete.

♦ He may be too distracted with everything going on around him, if you have a big interesting garden. Try restricting his access to all of it, use a lead if necessary.

♦ Go out more with him and give lots of praise and reward when he manages to get it right.

♦ Stay outside with him a bit longer and make sure you give him the opportunity to sniff about on his own.

♦ Be prepared – restrict his access when you come in, catch him in the act and correct him as detailed previously.

I reward my puppy for going outside but he still isn't getting the message

♦ He is still learning, be patient and persevere.

♦ Are you rewarding at the right time? Don't stand at the back door and reward him when he runs back to you. You will be rewarding for him for running back to the house, not for going to the toilet. Remember, a treat will reward your puppy for whatever he was doing when he is given it. Don't forget the one second rule.

♦ How often do you reward him for going outside? Try taking him out more often so you can reward him more often. Then he will get the message more quickly.

♦ Try changing your treats, use more tasty ones so he really remembers what he gets for going outside. Avoid using treats at other times until you have perfected the housetraining. This will make them more valuable so he will work harder.

My puppy won't run to me when I want to call him outside

♦ Try leaving a housetraining line attached, a lightweight 2m lead which you can leave on while at home (do not leave on while unattended). You should be able to pick up the lead and encourage him outside.

♦ Try waving a toy around or running outside yourself. This will make you more interesting and he will be more likely to want to run to you.

My puppy knows to go to the toilet outside but won't ask when the door is closed and just toilets in the house

◆ When your puppy really understands the housetraining principle, he will not want to go in the house. Look for signs that he wants to go outside. He may wait or hover by the back door, he may bark or whine at the door. He may get your attention and then turn and walk to the back door (trying to lead you there), he may scratch at the back door. Dogs have different methods of telling you and you need to watch and learn to recognise them. You could try not opening the door every time *you assume* he needs to go out and wait to see what he does.

◆ When he does let you know, make sure you praise him for *asking* to go outside.

My puppy always sneaks off to go somewhere in the house when I am not looking

◆ Restrict his access, he has too much freedom if he can do this.

◆ Stop telling him off for going to the toilet. Use the correct training procedure detailed previously.

◆ Use tastier treats and more praise when he does go outside.

My puppy seems to poo a lot of times in a day

◆ Check your feeding regime (chapter 1, feeding section). Remember what goes in, mostly comes out. Stick to set mealtimes or he will be constantly topping up and constantly emptying out.

♦ Maybe the food you are using does not agree with your puppy. It may be worth changing the brand – remember to change over gradually.

My puppy will only toilet on a puppy pad or newspaper

♦ Place the pad or newspaper outside to encourage him to go outside. Gradually move it further from the back door into the garden until he will naturally be attracted to go elsewhere.

My puppy will only toilet in my back garden and not when I am out on a walk

♦ Give it time, he is getting used to the big wide world.

♦ Use the same training procedures you used at home. Take treats with you and reward him for going outside.

♦ Let him see other dogs doing it outside, this may encourage him to do so himself.

♦ When his hormones kick in, he may naturally want to do this anyway to start leaving his scent around.

♦ Consider whether it is such a big deal. At least if he only does it at home, you should easily spot any problems should they occur.

This is a really common issue that owners raise, but most puppies will be happily toileting outside after a relatively short time.

My puppy was housetraining really well but suddenly has gone back to weeing in the house

♦ Lapses in progress are quite common during a puppy's first year. It may be caused by a change in circumstances or changes in growing and sexual maturity that your puppy is experiencing. If you experience this, stay calm, revert to the old training methods to reinforce the positive reward of going outside and you should overcome this successfully.

My puppy just wees all the time and doesn't seem to know he is doing it

♦ Take him to the vet. When a dog is constantly weeing while walking around, or doesn't get up from lying down to wee, there may be a medical problem you need help with. The most common cause is a urine infection which is often treated quite easily with antibiotics.

3

Barking, Whining and Attention Seeking

Attention seeking is an interesting topic and a subject which commonly comes up when meeting owners of puppies who are coming into adolescent age – that is, around five to six months old. Playing with your new puppy is great fun and many owners are only too happy to give lots of love and attention to their new little bundle of fluff. However, it is worth remembering that when you need to get back to normality, you won't be in the position to give your puppy all the attention they will have got used to in the early weeks. Neither should you give him attention all of the time. With most puppies, it is easy to avoid them becoming demanding of your attention as long as you handle it well in the first place.

Dogs do bark and so they should, but not for the wrong reasons. The information on barking in this chapter is relative to puppy training and not older dogs who have behaviour problems, that is a subject for another time, although hopefully you won't ever need to ask.

BARKING

You will probably learn to interpret your puppy's different noises. There are a number of ways dogs can communicate with us vocally and the chart below will give you an idea of what your dog's noises mean.

Barking	Why do dogs bark? It may be because they are looking for attention, they need something, are nervous or excited. It may be to let others – human or dogs – know they are there. Or they may simply bark after being barked at. If a dog is stressed or bored, this could also cause them to bark.
	Some breeds of dog were bred to bark. Some breeds will express themselves more vocally than others, such as smaller breeds. Commonly people think these smaller dogs bark more than bigger dogs and I would agree that they tend to, however, good training and socializing can often avoid them feeling the need to bark excessively.
	As with all areas of choosing a puppy, consider what your dog was bred for before choosing one who will be prone to behaviours that you know you will find hard to live with. Puppies don't bark immediately when they are born. Most puppies will have started to bark by the time they are two to three months old. Before a puppy barks, he will have learnt to whine to gain attention within the litter.

Whining   This is usually done for attention. It is the first sound a puppy will have learned to make within its litter.

It could also signal that your dog is worried or stressed.

Whimpering   This sounds more sorrowful than whining and can indicate pain or real misery.

Howling   We have all seen wolves howling on the television, or, if you are lucky enough, seen them for real. Howling is mainly a tool of communication. In the wild, dogs howl to let others know they are there. You don't often see domesticated dogs howling, but they can do it in response to other dogs barking or howling and they can do it if they are unhappy, or, most notably, lonely. Not many breeds are prone to howling, but in the pet world, the Basset Hound is probably the most likely to do this.

Yelping   This is done as a result of pain. It is normally a short sharp bark which signals that your dog has been hurt.

Growling   You need to distinguish between different types of growling. Puppies often make growly noises when they are playing. It is all part of them growing up and learning about themselves. Lots of dogs make these noises when playing tug of war, they are just getting involved in the game. However, if you don't want your dog to make these sounds, simply end the game and walk away immediately when they begin making any noise. This teaches them to avoid making noises while playing, otherwise, the play will end. Often, dogs may moan, softly and deeply while you are stroking or cuddling them. This is a sign of pleasure and is nothing to worry about.

Aggressive growling is different. The growl will be low and

steady and is a warning to you to back away. This growl may
come if a dog is nervous and stressed and his body language
will often be stiff without movement.

Snarling   Snarling will follow growling. If you don't react to the original
growl, then the growl becomes more fierce. It will be louder
and less steady and the lips will be curled up and the teeth will
be bared. If your dog reaches this stage, it means that you will
probably see aggressive behaviour next, and generally pretty
quickly.

ATTENTION SEEKING

How can I prevent attention seeking problems?

1. With your new puppy, start as you mean to go on. Be realistic
    about giving attention. Your puppy needs to learn that he
    gets attention when you want to give it and not the other way
    around.

    Remember: as pack leader, you need to be in control of
    everything.

2. When your puppy comes looking for attention, don't always
    give it. Without even realizing, many owners stroke and
    respond to their puppy's request for attention every single
    time they ask for it. This is a sure way to ensure your puppy
    gets what he wants, when he wants it. When your puppy
    comes to you for fuss and attention, make sure that some of
    the time you ignore him. Do this by:

a) Break eye contact, do not talk or touch him.

b) Turn your back on him.

c) Stand up and leave the room.

Either way, use this body language to communicate that you won't play with him at this time.

It is extremely important that you are firm with your own behaviour.

Remember: even looking at your puppy will give him attention. In order to ignore effectively, you must not look at him.

3. When you are playing with your puppy, be the one who ends the game sometimes. Don't always wait for him to get bored. Gain some authority by saying 'I've had enough!' Communicate this simply by using your body language.

    When you have finished playing, stand up, break eye contact and walk away.

4. If your puppy is stealing things to get your attention, *do not* enter into a chase to try and get them back. If you start chasing your puppy, he will learn what fun it is and will continue to steal to have more fun.

5. Restrict your puppy's ability to follow you around the house. This is useful to prevent separation issues but is also good practise to avoid him trying to get your attention all the time (and to avoid you being duped into giving it willingly).

Remember: If you have ignored your puppy to avoid attention seeking, make sure that he is happily playing or settled on his own before you return and give any attention.

Always ask yourself who is in control of a situation. If it is always your puppy, then you should rethink your own behaviour.

What do I do if my puppy is attention seeking?

Barking and whining

Examples of attention seeking barking include the following.

♦ You are sitting on the sofa watching television and your puppy walks up in front of you, stands and barks at you.

♦ You are talking on the phone or have stopped on the street to talk to someone and your puppy starts barking.

♦ Your puppy brings you a toy and 'demands' that you throw it for them.

♦ Your puppy stands in between you and your visitors and tries to be the 'centre of attention'.

If your puppy is barking at you for attention, don't give it. Remember that mostly dogs will only 'demand' attention if they have worked out how to obtain it. Your puppy learns by association. 'If I bark at my owner, they give me some attention'. Therefore, if you take away the attention, your puppy will learn to stop barking at you, because there is no reward for the behaviour.

> Whenever you look at a dog's behaviour, there will be a consequence to the action. If you want to change the behaviour, you need to change the consequence.

If your puppy is barking at you for attention, then he has already learnt that this behaviour will get him the result. Even negative attention is rewarding for most puppies, so even if you are telling him to 'be quiet', he may still be happy to be getting some attention from you.

When your puppy barks at you
When your puppy barks at you, do the following.

♦ Break eye contact, turn your back on him and walk away.

♦ *Do not* look, talk, touch or acknowledge your puppy in any way.

This will teach your puppy that he will not get attention by barking. Don't forget to give him some attention when he isn't demanding it. This will teach him that he gets fun and games when he doesn't have rude manners.

When your puppy barks at visitors
Remove your dog from the area. If he is barking and 'playing up' while you have visitors, place him in another room. However, if your puppy is barking and behaving nervously rather than barking for attention, then you should seek professional advice.

If he is barking *at* your visitors for attention, walk him into the room on a lead and the second he barks, remove him. Repeat this over and over until he understands that barking will produce an undesirable result.

Stealing

If your puppy is stealing to get your attention, then, again, he has already learnt that this will entice you into a game. Some puppies think it is fun to make you chase after them and in order to change this behaviour – you need to stop chasing. Here are some methods you can try:

- Look in the training section and learn how to teach your puppy to 'leave'. The best way to deal with problems like this is to stop them occurring in the first place. Teaching your puppy a command to stop them stealing in the first place is by far my preferred method.

  Remember, if he does 'leave' when you ask, reward him with something else – perhaps a treat or a toy.

- If the item your puppy has stolen is not valuable or dangerous, then ignore the fact he has stolen it. Try distraction. Ignore your puppy, get up and do something interesting yourself that he will want to come and join in with, i.e. start playing with a ball, bounce it and kick it, all the while ignoring your dog. When he comes to play, let him join in.

- If the item is valuable or dangerous and you need to get it back quickly, use a treat to get it back. You need to use a treat of high value, i.e. something worth giving up the item for. If you can approach your puppy without him running off, then hold out a treat in the palm of your hand and 'exchange' it for whatever he has stolen.

Remember to use the word ' leave' as he drops the item he has stolen.

Keep the usual items he steals out of reach while you are training him to leave and to break the habits already in place. You should try to avoid having to use treats as much as possible to avoid the risk of him being rewarded for stealing.

♦ Use a house training line and leave it attached to your dog to trail while in the house. This is a lightweight lead which you can pick up when necessary for training or correcting behaviour. When your dog steals and runs off, you can avoid the 'chase' by reeling him in and removing the item from him. Do this every time and he will soon get bored of stealing.

TIP

I meet many puppies who love to steal and often they are active breeds, such as Spaniels or other breeds who love to work. You need to assess your puppy's activity levels and, if necessary, increase his stimulation by walking, playing and training. While dogs mostly steal for attention, my experience is that this is often because they are bored.

4

Biting, Chewing and Jumping

BITING

Why your puppy bites

Play biting or 'mouthing' is a normal puppy behaviour. Much like babies, puppies explore with their mouths. They will learn about texture, noise and the capabilities of their jaws. Most puppies will learn about biting and how much it hurts while with their litter.

Chewing is different from biting. Your puppy will be teething. He will have an urge to 'chew' to help relieve his teeth and gums while they are growing, his baby teeth fall out and the new adult ones come through. Puppies will also chew on things if they are bored or have learned this is a good way to get your attention.

Bite-inhibition

You need to practise bite-inhibition with your puppy. Bite-inhibition involves ensuring your puppy is aware of what damage his teeth and jaws can do. This is important for you to reinforce, not only to help you now, but also for when your puppy gets older. If he is not aware of what damage he *could* do, if he ever needs to give a warning bite or nip, he may do a lot of damage unintentionally, because he didn't know he could.

The methods detailed here are the most effective and most useful. If you use different punishing methods you may cause problems with your puppy becoming frightened of you handling them around their mouth. Teeth cleaning, removing objects or giving pills could become a problem. We don't want to teach puppies not to accept our hands around their mouths, we just want to teach them not to bite on them.

Stopping your puppy biting and teaching bite-inhibition
Your aim is to do the following.

♦ Teach your puppy that they cannot bite on you (or anyone else).

♦ Teach your puppy to play with toys (with or without you).

♦ Teach your puppy that if he bites on you, you will stop playing.

The way to do it is:

1. When your puppy bites on you, yell 'ouch', pull your arm away, step back and hold the bitten area as if you are really

hurt (of course, you really might be). At the same time, look your puppy in the face. After only a couple of seconds, continue playing, using toys to encourage him to bite and play with them.

2. If however, your puppy comes straight back and bites you again, stand up, turn your back on him, do not look at him or talk to him and leave the room. After one minute, return and continue as normal.

3. If your puppy goes into a biting frenzy, and walking away just means he runs after you and carries on jumping and biting at you, *calmly* take him to another room – a 'time-out' zone – place him there and turn and walk away. After one minute, return to him, let him out and start over again.

IMPORTANT POINTS TO REMEMBER

When you practise these techniques there are important points to remember.

♦   Do not look at your puppy unless it says to do so.

♦   Do not talk to your puppy unless it says to do so.

♦   If you need to use a time-out, you must enforce it when your puppy is biting you, not after you have spent five minutes trying to catch him.

Hanging off your clothes

This problem is slightly different, in that your puppy isn't biting on you, but normally on an item of clothing. Most commonly, trousers, skirts, dressing gowns and shoelaces. The principle of correction is the same although we don't yell 'ouch' because generally it is ineffective in this situation and your puppy hasn't hurt you.

If your puppy is chasing after your clothing, you need to distract him onto something else.

1. Stop and stand still.

2. Interrupt the behaviour by clapping your hands or making a short, sharp disapproving noise.

3. Encourage your puppy onto a toy instead of your clothes.

4. If he won't leave you alone, take him immediately to the time-out zone.

5. In severe cases, you could use a squirt of water to interrupt this behaviour. Only do so if the other methods aren't working for you. You should ensure that your puppy does not know where the water came from and that you do not get into a confrontational position with him. This means, you would squirt the water to stop the behaviour, and then turn and walk away or offer a toy to distract him. Using negative techniques when training puppies isn't my preference, and I would only do this if after following the correct procedures, a puppy really isn't responding.

Biting the children

The methods detailed here are the same for everybody. However, sometimes puppies will play bite more with children because they are smaller, have less authority and are generally more exciting because they run around and make a lot of noise.

If your child is old enough to follow the above procedures properly themselves, then let them do so.

If your child is too young, then *you* must follow the procedures for them. Tell your child to stand completely still and then intervene using the distracting techniques or time-out response as appropriate. Never leave a child alone with your puppy to avoid this problem getting out of hand. I have met many children who have got scared of their puppy and don't want to come into the room while he is there. Don't let this happen in your family.

Never leave children and dogs alone and make sure you deal with the play biting immediately.

A good training aid to use when children are around is a house training line. This is a lightweight lead, two metres long, which your puppy wears in the house. This is useful, because to interrupt a behaviour, you can pick up the lead and correct your puppy away from your clothes or your children. When he has stopped biting and calmed down, you can praise and try relaxing the lead again.

How long does it take to stop the biting?

As a general rule, in my experience, you should see an improvement within a few days and you should find it completely stopped within two to three weeks. Exceptions to this rule are those puppies with a very severe biting problem or those living with owners who don't follow the correct training procedure (or do follow the rules, but only for a couple of days).

Time-out zone

If you need to use a time-out zone, you should choose an area where your puppy will not automatically be distracted onto playing with something else in there.

Using the garden or a room where there are toys or items of yours always lying around to be played with or chewed up is not a good idea. Many people use a downstairs toilet, a utility room or spare room they have prepared earlier. The kitchen or hall could also be used. If these are simply not an option, invest in a sturdy puppy pen which you can leave up and ready for when you need it. Needless to say, don't leave toys in there.

The point of using time-out is to communicate to your puppy that his biting you was so unacceptable that you are refusing to play with him. This is a disaster as far as a puppy is concerned because they hate it when you ignore them and won't play anymore. No punishment is more effective so forget about shouting and tapping him on the nose, etc.

Remember: If you need to use time-out, never return to release your puppy if he is barking or whining while 'timing-out'. If you do this, he will learn that creating lots of noise makes you come and let him out.

COMMON PROBLEMS AND SOLUTIONS TO BITING

Can I use his crate as the time-out zone?

♦ No, you should avoid using a crate as a punishment zone. If the crate is used as a sleeping area and your puppy is happy to settle in there, then using it as a punishment zone will probably lead him to not wanting to go in there at all.

I just can't encourage my puppy onto a toy instead

• You should have a good variety of toys. Don't leave them around all the time, make sure you rotate them to make them more interesting. Remember that something which is accessible all the time becomes boring, why would your puppy go and play with it now when these shoelaces are so much more fun? After all, he can always get the toy later.

• Using squeaky or noisy toys are better for distractions because they will help get your puppy's attention. Suitable chew toys which have some flavour are also useful for this. Try using a 'treat' on a toy, such as a little puppy chicken paste, to make it more attractive. If your puppy remembers that these toys are rewarding, he will be more easily distracted by them.

• Don't forget to interrupt your puppy first, going straight for a distraction makes it harder. As with any training, get your dog's attention first by clapping or using a short, sharp vocal noise such as 'Aahh' to correct him. Follow up with your distraction or command.

I yelled 'ouch' but my puppy didn't take any notice at all

You are probably not yelling loudly or painfully enough. It should be a short, sharp yelp. You are looking to obtain a reaction. When you 'ouch', your puppy should back off and look at you, even if only for a second. This way you know that he has taken your displeasure on board. Improve your 'ouch' so it works better next time.

I have practised these methods for ages but my puppy is still biting

There may be one of these reasons for this.

◆ It's quite rare, but you may have a very severe case of biting to deal with. I have met a few puppies that just bite and bite and bite. Praising them for playing with toys is extremely difficult because they may only do it for a second before they are biting you again. If you have a really severe case, try using the housetraining line I mentioned earlier to correct your puppy. Use a variety of toys and regularly change them so your puppy may find something new and interesting, giving you longer time to praise and building up more time to differentiate between right and wrong. These puppies get over it eventually but I understand it is extremely frustrating, just persevere and they do get the message. It just takes a little longer. You should also find, that when your puppy can go out for walks and training, this problem will improve a lot with the extra activity and stimulation. If you are not making any progress, seek further advice because you may need help to use a different correction and in establishing better hierarchy as well.

♦ Your timing. You are simply not reacting quickly enough and dealing with the biting every time it happens. Remember that you have one second to correct a dog's behaviour. Basically, if your puppy is not corrected *while* he is biting, then you are not communicating effectively enough. If you need to use a time out, you must take him just as he is biting, not when he has finished.

♦ You (or someone), is rough playing with your puppy. If you encourage rough play, that is, you allow your puppy to jump all over you, biting and chewing on you, then you only have yourselves to blame. Rough play teaches your puppy that this type of play is acceptable, and so he will then do it to others and quite likely, the dogs that he plays with in the park. Put a stop to this type of play immediately.

♦ You have given up too early. Often, you will need to continue with a method for a good two weeks before your puppy will understand your message. They need to make the 'link' – 'Aahh, every time I do this, then that happens'. When a puppy learns the consequence of a behaviour, that is when you will see him consciously start to become aware of and think about his actions.

CHEWING

Why does my puppy chew?

Puppies explore with their mouths. They will pick things up to feel their texture. They will taste all manner of items, including those you'd rather they didn't, and then they may, unfortunately, proceed to chew them up. So why do they do this? Well, aside from the exploring factors, puppies will of course, be teething.

Teething

Much like a baby, a puppy will have an almost uncontrollable urge to bite and chew to relieve their discomfort. A puppy will be teething and losing their baby teeth, normally from around four months old, you may even find some of them around the home. Often, this teething process can last until a puppy is seven months old, after which the need to chew subsides and owners can breathe a huge sigh of relief. This is until they start all over again with the next stage of teething, which is the adult teeth adjusting position in the jaws and setting themselves in for adult life.

I often speak to owners of 10 to 11 month old dogs who advise me that their dog was fine, had stopped chewing but is suddenly doing it again even more and wrecking their home. These are classic cases of being lulled into a false sense of security. The owners have given their dog more freedom and he is now well used to not staying in a crate or pen when they go out. Well, you have been warned! My advice is don't give too much freedom to your dog, until you are sure that they can be trusted: Generally by the time they are one, teething will be complete.

Stopping your puppy chewing

You can't stop your puppy chewing. A puppy will need to chew as explained above. However, what you can do is teach your puppy not to chew on things he shouldn't.

You can restrict your puppy's access, using a crate or puppy pen while you are out. This will avoid him chewing up your home and avoid you getting angry with him when you return. However, in order to teach a puppy what he can and can't chew on, you need to get him in your environment to learn. You should supervise your puppy to ensure he doesn't cause any damage and so that you can correct him from chewing those things that he shouldn't.

Remember that as with most puppy behaviours, it isn't about telling your puppy off, it's about teaching what is acceptable. They simply won't know that they can't chew up your whole house unless you teach them.

The simplest way to correct is to:

1. Interrupt

2. Distract

In order to encourage your puppy to chew something suitable you must first get his attention so you can direct him.

You can interrupt his behaviour by clapping your hands, making a sharp noise with your voice, squeaking a toy, in fact, anything which will make him turn and look at you. Once you get his attention, you can offer a suitable alternative for your puppy to chew on. Keep repeating this over and over. By providing a consistent interruption, it shouldn't take long before your puppy knows what he can and can't chew on.

COMMON PROBLEMS AND SOLUTIONS TO CHEWING

I interrupt my puppy but he ignores the toy and carries on chewing

♦ Maybe your toy isn't good enough. Remember to keep toys interesting by only leaving out a few at a time. Too many toys or the same old toys become boring. Keep your puppy interested in toys by not letting him have access to them all of the time and rotating when they come out to play.

♦ Try toys of a different texture that may be more appealing to your puppy.

♦ Try toys which make a noise, 'squeaky' or 'babble' toys can be more fun.

♦ Toys stuffed with food are also very attractive.

♦ Try using a housetraining line, so you can actually remove your puppy from the area and focus him on his toys.

My puppy keeps returning to the same piece of furniture to chew

♦ Your puppy has already learnt that chewing in this place is rewarding. In order to prevent this, you must correct him immediately he starts, not five minutes after he has started chewing. Try spraying the area with anti-chew or bitter apple spray, both designed to taste horrible and so deter your puppy from chewing in this area.

♦ If possible, you may like to move the item out of reach/access for a while. Puppies often return to the same spot if chewing has proved rewarding there previously. Don't forget that dogs are very habit forming. Removing the item for a while will help to break this habit while you continue training.

♦ Try using a housetraining line. As you correct your puppy, say 'leave' and then encourage him to chew on a toy.

Remember to always react in a calm manner. Providing you don't leave your puppy unattended, he shouldn't cause any damage within the home. Like anything, it will need you to repeat the correction over and over until your puppy understands. He is young and will forget until he is shown enough times. Once or twice isn't good enough and each puppy will vary in terms of how quickly they understand. However, providing you are consistent and don't leave him unattended, you will probably communicate your message within two to four weeks. Remember though, that you shouldn't give your puppy too much freedom when you are out. At this young age, he may still forget the rules if you go out and leave him to it.

JUMPING

Why does my puppy jump up?

An excited puppy who is pleased to see you will often jump all over you. If you watch, he will normally be jumping up towards your face. This is because your face is you, it is your personality. It is often where he will get attention from and he knows it. Your face is one of the highest points on your body and so your puppy will need to jump to get there. Jumping up is nearly always an attention seeking behaviour.

Stopping your puppy jumping up at you

This is actually quite simple. It is a matter of dealing with the end result. In fact, whenever you are looking to change your puppy's behaviour, you need to look at the end result, rather than the behaviour itself. If you change the consequence to the action, then the action/behaviour will change.

What is my puppy gaining from the jumping up?
Answer: Attention

Coming into the house or getting up in the morning
Your puppy has been missing you and is pleased to see you. When he comes rushing over to jump up at you do the following.

1. Fold your arms across your chest to create a mock barrier between your face and your puppy.

2. Stand tall and upright – do not bend down.

3. Break eye contact – *do not* look at your puppy. Look up if it helps but do not look down.

4. Turn away from your puppy who will probably be jumping at the front of you.

5. If your puppy rushes back around to the front of you, turn your back on him again.

6. When your puppy has all four feet on the floor, you can
    then acknowledge him and say 'hello', even offer a treat to
    reinforce the good behaviour. If he starts to jump again, stand
    up and begin at point one again.

If you take away the attention, your puppy will learn that jumping
up doesn't get him what he was looking for. A dog won't continue
a behaviour like this if there is no point to it. Therefore, the
jumping will stop when he has made this realization.

Stopping your puppy jumping up at others
Hopefully you will clearly see how removing attention will stop
your puppy from jumping all over you. These methods don't work
in exactly the same way with visitors or people you meet outside.
The principle is the same but you will encounter problems with
others allowing your puppy to jump up at them.

Have we all met 'Mrs I don't mind', 'Mr Dogs love me' and 'Miss
I'm used to it'? These well intentioned members of the public can
cause real problems to puppy owners, allowing dogs to jump all
over them, praising and rewarding them at the same time. This
simply teaches puppies that they can jump over all manner of
people and it is perfectly acceptable. Well, it isn't, and it is up to
you to train your puppy out of this anti-social behaviour.

At home
My experience is that when you ask visitors to your house to
ignore your jumping puppy, they don't all do it. While I know this
isn't true of everybody, there is a high percentage of people who
feel obliged to stroke or acknowledge your puppy in spite of you
asking them not to. With this in mind, you need to deal with the

jumping up yourself. Don't rely on others to do it for you: it very rarely works and your puppy is *your* responsibility anyway.

1. When visitors enter your home, your puppy needs to be on a lead. Either
   a) Put him on a lead before you open the door
   b) Keep him in another room until your visitor is in the house and then put his lead on before you bring him in to meet your visitor.

2. Let your puppy go and say hello. Do not pull him back with the lead. You *must* keep the lead loose and you need to stay relaxed yourself.

3. Don't say anything to your puppy other than calmly praise him if he is saying hello nicely with all four feet on the ground.

4. If your puppy jumps up at your visitor, use your lead to calmly pull him away *immediately* when he jumps. Turn your back on your visitors and walk him away to completely remove him from the attention. Don't just pull him back a few feet from your visitor as he will simply keep pulling on the lead to get there again. This would not be clearly communicating that his jumping has caused him to be removed from the interaction. Walking away will put you in the position of completely removing your dog from the attention, thus giving him the same result as previously when working on your own.

5. When your puppy is calm, you can walk him back over to the visitor and start again. Use the same procedure over and over until your puppy learns that jumping stops the fun.

Outside

It is the case that if you teach your puppy that jumping at people indoors is not acceptable, then this will have some knock-on effect outside. With all training, if you cannot get your puppy to behave as you like indoors, you don't stand much chance of achieving good behaviour outside.

When walking along the street and your puppy starts lunging to jump at a passer-by do the following.

1. Tell your puppy to 'Leave'.

2. Speed up.

3. Walk on past (without your puppy getting to the passer-by).

   You must teach your puppy that he *cannot* jump at people outside. This is quite hard for owners to do when 'Mrs I don't mind' wants to stop and say hello, but you must be firm. Remember, the next passer-by may be an elderly person or young child whom your boisterous puppy could easily knock over.

   When out in the park, if your puppy runs at people or children and jumps up at them, you should keep him on a long line or tracking lead to keep control. This way, you can adopt the previous method of using a lead to correct your puppy if he is going to jump up at people.

> **TIP**
> When teaching your puppy to 'leave' and walk past other
> people or dogs like this, remember to let him stop and say
> 'hello' to some. Otherwise, you may cause social problems.
> The point of the exercise is to teach manners, that is to
> walk past calmly or if you permit – to stop and say hello.

At any occasion, you can teach your puppy that if they sit, then
they will be rewarded with a treat. When you are outside or have
visitors to your home, you can provide them with a treat and ask
them to tell your puppy to sit and offer him the treat when he
is doing so. This method may work with some puppies and it is
worth practising, however, it is not my preferred method. I have
met too many puppies who sit for their treat and then proceed to
jump up afterwards. This shows that the puppy is learning to sit
for a treat, not to stop jumping up. In my experience, removing
attention as detailed earlier is more effective for a long-term
result.

Stopping your puppy jumping on other dogs

You will notice that some dogs play rougher than others. You
should find as a general rule that most dogs will offer a puppy
licence: this means that they will be very tolerant of younger dogs
bouncing around and on them to play. However, when puppies
reach five to six months old, they may start to get some warnings
from the older dogs who will not allow them to continue this
rough play for much longer. Likewise, there are plenty of dogs
out there who enjoy running around with the younger ones and
are happy to encourage boisterous play because they enjoy it

themselves. As time goes on, your puppy will learn social skills from these other dogs and he will learn to interpret which dogs don't want to play and which ones really do.

I think that as far as play goes, you should draw the line at them jumping onto another dog's back. Again, other dogs will help your puppy learn that this isn't acceptable. They may give a growl or 'see them off' which should help your puppy start to be more conscious of their own behaviour.

An adult dog mounting another is often a sign of dominance and you can help your puppy avoid getting into trouble with others by correcting play which you deem unacceptable. If you correct your puppy, it will also help your hierarchy as your puppy will see you asserting your authority outside.

If your puppy is jumping on the back of another dog, particularly one who would rather he wasn't, simply walk over and pull him off. Be calm and confident. You can say 'no' at the same time.

If he repeats the behaviour, simply pull him off again. If the problem is persistent and your puppy ignores these corrections, put him on the lead and walk him away. Don't allow him to keep getting away with ignoring you.

If your puppy is running a good distance away from you and playing rough and jumping on the back of other dogs, you should be keeping him on the lead until you reach dogs that are suitable for him to play with. This will keep you in control, because you need to be with your puppy if you are going to be able to correct him, not to mention the fact that if your puppy is running some distance away from you, you should be stopping this happening anyway.

Is he jumping or humping?

As your puppy becomes an adolescent and testosterone levels in his body increase you may start to notice your dog humping. You may notice play jumping lead into humping and you may even see it in females too. Often when your dog is overexcited, this humping may begin – the first sign being your dog mounting on the back of another. Alternatively, the humping may be a sign of your dog wanting to dominate another. Many dogs don't take kindly to this activity so this is another reason you should discourage any form of jumping on another dog's back from an early age.

Your dog may also take to humping on your leg. Watch out for this, as it is commonly a dominance issue and you may need to look at your pack hierarchy.

How long does it take to stop my puppy jumping?

An expected timescale for stopping your puppy jumping at you would be around two weeks. You may notice that in the first two to three days of you ignoring him, his jumping may get worse. This is because he is doing something which has worked previously and because he is not getting a response from you, he will think you suddenly cannot see him. It can also be a kind of protest, your puppy making a lot of fuss at the changes you are putting into place. In order to rectify this problem, he may jump higher and longer than before, but this will only last for a day or two.

At this point, many owners think that the methods aren't working and give up, but you must persevere. Keep up with the training for two weeks (and be consistent) and you should be on top of this problem. Jumping up is an area of training which will benefit from all owners following the same rules. Chances are, if only one member of the house follows the rules and the others don't, your puppy's jumping behaviour won't improve.

For jumping at visitors or people outside, it may take a little longer to stop the jumping. This is simply because usually you won't be able to practise as often. Don't forget you can set up situations to practise. The more you practise, the quicker he will learn. Why not get friends and family to turn up at the park, as your puppy runs to jump at them they could use the ignoring methods you have been using at home. You could also ask them to keep visiting your house, ringing the doorbell and coming into the house, giving you the opportunity to practise correcting your puppy's greetings.

COMMON PROBLEMS AND SOLUTIONS TO JUMPING

I have tried everything but my puppy is still jumping

There may be a couple of reasons for this.

1. You may not have persevered long enough with your training. Don't give in too easily. Remember, normally two weeks of consistently following the training methods should see a good improvement, although puppies will vary in their ability to learn.

2. Your timing is poor. You must ignore and praise at exactly the right time. Even one second either way can give the wrong message to your puppy. Don't be tempted to 'let him get away with it this time'. That's all he will need to get away with it the next time.

5

Pack Hierarchy

TOP DOG

It is likely that you will have heard the expression 'Top Dog'. This is a term people can use in everyday language. I am referring in this book however, to avoiding your canine companion getting too big for his boots and beginning to take over your household.

Establishing a stable hierarchy within your house is extremely important. Dogs are pack animals and need to be sure of their position within their pack. If you fail to give clear direction and establish yourself as the leader of your pack, then your puppy may work his way up the ranks to a position higher than yours.

If this happens, there are many behaviour problems that may arise as your puppy develops into an adolescent dog.

It is important to remember that most dogs don't actually want to be top dog. Most are actually happier to be a part of the pack, with someone else having the responsibility of looking after things. Poor leadership from owners however, means many dogs get given jobs that they can't handle and they can end up feeling quite stressed and unhappy.

This section is probably the most important in this book. It will help you see how to give your puppy a secure and stable pack environment while keeping you as Number One.

THE HIERARCHY IN YOUR HOUSE

Basically, any humans in your house should be more important than your dog. If your dog sees himself as more important than any member of your house, then you may end up having to deal with behaviour problems.

PROBLEMS THAT MAY OCCUR WHEN PACK HIERARCHY IS NOT RIGHT

- ◆ Your dog may do what one person says, but ignores other family members.

- ◆ Your dog may see some members of your household as 'playmates'.

- ◆ Your dog may not relax within your house and appears unsettled, often getting up and down and pacing around.

- Your dog may bark at people walking past your house or coming to your front door. He may take to barking or chasing at things moving around outside, such as birds, the wind through the trees or any sudden movements that make them jump.

- Your dog may react nervously or aggressively towards other dogs.

- You may find your dog reluctant to 'give up' his seat on the sofa for you and will even become aggressive towards you if you try to move him!

- Your dog may be possessive over his food, growling or snapping at anyone who comes close to it.

- If you allow your dog to sleep on your bed, then he may not let others get in or will growl at you if you move about and disturb him.

- Your dog may urinate around your house, even on your bed!

- Your dog may have little respect for you, ignoring your commands and choosing to do as he pleases.

HOW TO ACHIEVE THE CORRECT HIERARCHY WITHIN YOUR PACK

- Do not allow your puppy to ignore your commands. If you say 'sit' make sure he does it!

- Treat all humans in the house as more important than your puppy. When you come home, say hello to your family first and then greet your puppy.

◆ Do not override other members of the family. If your puppy isn't listening to another member of the house, let them persevere until they get the desired response from him. Do not 'butt' in and make him do it yourself. This would teach your puppy that the other family member isn't that important and they don't have to do what they say.

◆ All humans must have privileges your puppy doesn't have. By not allowing your puppy on the furniture or upstairs, then you have things you can do and places you can go which your puppy can't. This will help him see you all as more important than him within your pack.

◆ Do not walk or sneak around your puppy if he is in the way or blocking your path. Even from this young age, make your puppy get up and move out of your way or step over him to assert your authority.

◆ Do not allow your puppy to demand attention from you. If your puppy keeps coming over for fuss and attention, DO NOT give it. Teach your puppy that he cannot demand attention whenever he chooses.

◆ If you are playing with your puppy, be the one who ends the interaction first. Before he gets fed up of the game and chooses to walk away, be the one to end it first by walking away yourself.

◆ If you are playing tug games with your puppy, you must win most (not all) of them. However, dogs of a competitive nature should not be encouraged to play competitive games.

- Teach your puppy to sit and wait for his dinner. Give him permission before you allow him to eat it.

- Never leave food down for a dog to eat when he chooses. This will make it his food which he may feel prone to defend. Food should always be seen as yours which you are in control of (see more details below).

- Get children involved in feeding, it will help elevate their position in the pack by being in control of his food.

- Act like a leader, be calm, assertive and in control all of the time. If you display fear or nervousness in any situation, your puppy will become fearful of it too. If you are weak and submissive, as he matures, your puppy will start to take control. If you are inconsistent, noisy and too physical in your handling, that is arms and legs all over the place or pushing and pulling your puppy around, then your puppy will be over active like this too.

FEEDING

There are only a few things of much value to a dog and food is often quite high up on the list.

It is important that you remain in control of your puppy's food so that he will grow up to accept that it is your food and not his!

When a dog sees food as their own, it can lead to food related behaviour problems and may also be a contributing factor to poor hierarchy within a home.

How To Feed Your Dog

♦ Feed your dog but only allow half an hour for him to eat it. After this time, remove what is not eaten and do not return the food until the next mealtime. For young puppies, judge the situation before becoming too strict with this: i.e. if your young puppy has been ill he may start feeding again little and often. Follow your vet's advice if special circumstances apply.

♦ Feed your puppy after humans. This may sometimes be difficult at first because puppies often have numerous meals a day. As your puppy reaches five to six months old this should be easier to stick with all the time. The leader of the pack would always eat first.

♦ Don't allow your puppy to charge in and scoff all the food within a second of it being put down. Teach some manners by making your puppy sit and look at you until you give permission to go ahead and eat it. This may be hard at first with a young puppy who is excited for his dinner, but keep at it! Use a lead to help you if necessary.

♦ Don't allow your puppy food without working for it. Only use treats for training exercises only. If your puppy receives treats and titbits all the time, it will make him far less likely to work for them when you really want him to.

♦ To prevent your puppy from guarding his food – keep a little food back at mealtimes and while your puppy is eating, approach him and add this food to his bowl. This will teach him that people approaching his food bowl while he is eating is a good thing as it will often lead to more food. Don't be tempted to keep on taking his food away while he is eating.

While doing this occasionally is fine, if you do it too much you may find your puppy simply grows annoyed with you keep interrupting his meal. This can lead to him becoming aggressive with you, a behaviour problem which could easily have been avoided. Imagine how annoying it would be if someone kept on removing your dinner while you were trying to eat it.

♦ If you have a puppy who gulps his food down in a second you can try to slow him down. These ideas will be great for mental stimulation too:

— Feed some meals in toys designed for stuffing with food – they will release the food slowly.

— Feed his meals in a few bowls, so he moves from one to the other to prevent him from gulping his whole meal down in one.

— Lay out a food hunt or trail. This will slow him down due to the time involved in 'hunting'.

BODY LANGUAGE

Body Language is a great way of communicating with your puppy. I have detailed here some advice on Body Language that you can use to communicate with your puppy and also some comments on what a dog's body language is telling you! I always try to make owners aware of their body language when training. If you give out the wrong signals to your dog, it can affect their behaviour tremendously. You may be saying one thing but your dog may be seeing another!

Your Body Language

This table shows how your dog interprets your body language.

What you are doing:	What you are saying:
Shouting at your dog to stop barking at something	'I am joining in with you'
Crouching down, cuddling your dog to reassure him because you think he is nervous or 'going to' be nervous of a situation	'Gosh, this is really scary isn't it! Let's huddle together and hopefully we will be ok!'
Picking your dog up because you are worried that the dog approaching is going to frighten him	'That dog approaching us is really bad! – be afraid of it'
Stroking, petting and comforting your dog during or just after he has displayed any form of behaviour that is undesirable – even nervousness	'That's right – I like that behaviour'
Getting up and looking out of the window to see who your dog is barking at, telling him to be quiet and/or stroking & touching him	'Who is that out there? Oh yes, I can see, thanks for letting me know!'
Greeting your dog before other humans in the house	'You are more important to me than they are'
Doing nothing when your dog ignores you	'That's ok, you do what you like, you don't have to listen to me!'

Your dog's body language

There are general indicators with a dog's body language as to
how they are feeling. It can be hard to accurately diagnose a
dog's body language because it can be over with very quickly.
You will also notice that some actions appear in more than one
place here, so it is important to remember that you should watch
and look at *all* the signals. This information isn't so relevant to
young puppies, but you may find it interesting as they grow older
or when looking at the behaviour of other dogs you may meet on
your travels. I have, however, met dogs which seem to give off
one signal which doesn't fit with the behaviour. For example, the
hackles being raised when the dog is clearly happy and excited
rather than nervous or aggressive. It would seem, in this instance,
that the excitement of the occasion has provoked an involuntary
reaction and the dog is simply overexcited. A wagging tail does
not always mean a happy dog, it depends on the type of wag.
Check below for more details.

Aggressive body language

The dog is normally still, maybe leaning slightly forward and
staring at you. His hackles will be raised and his forehead may be
wrinkled. His lips will be drawn forward/upwards and the teeth
may be bared. His tail will be quite still, the same as his overall
body and it will point straight out, or it may be extended and
curved clearly indicating an aggressive demeanour.

Friendly/relaxed body language

Happy tail wagging is shown by big wide movements from side
to side. Often, you will see your dog's bum wiggle with the wag if
he is really happy! Ears will be laid back and his forehead will be
smooth and relaxed.

Confident/alert/interested body language

The ears will be pointed up (or as pointy as they can be if your dog has floppy ones!). The tail will be held high and still or may have a slight wag that seems to almost flick if not completely confident. He may be staring and his eyebrows may be raised. He will hold himself upright with a straight back and will be holding his head high.

Nervous body language

The ears are laid back, the tail is still and low or between the legs. The dog may be crouching, lifting a paw, and there may be slightly closed (or blinking) eyes or licking of the lips. If a dog shows you his stomach by lying down and turning over after displaying these signals, then this is not an invitation to tickle his tummy, it is the dog communicating that he is not happy for you to approach so 'please leave me alone!'

His hackles may be raised which is generally an involuntary action as a result of the way he is feeling.

A dog may bare his teeth when nervous as well, the lips being drawn backwards to display the teeth, rather than the forwards/upwards movement when a dog is being aggressive.

If your dog stands quite still and goes quite stiff, he may just be waiting for the 'threat' to go away. If the threat still approaches, the chances are the dog will react badly.

Submissive body language

This will be similar to a nervous dogs body language. There may be other signals you notice such as your dog showing another his throat by turning his head away to the side. This is to signal that he is not a threat to the other dog by putting this vulnerable part of his body on show. Other submissive gestures are indicated by having a curled back, perhaps crouching low and possibly circling himself down into a completely submissive position on the floor.

Yawning and Scratching	This is often a 'stress reliever'. I see it a lot in puppy classes when the puppies are coping with the new regime of training. Also, yawning is a calming signal and you can do it to show your puppy you are quite calm and relaxed.
Circling	Dogs do this often before they settle to sleep or before toileting. I have met dogs which circle madly with excitement or others who do it because they are stressed or bored and have made it into a habit.
Sniffing	This is a dog's primary activity, many can sniff and sniff and sniff. It's what they do, but they may also use this activity as a calming signal to others. It can have the same effect as yawning to show disinterest and that they are not threatening.

Part 2

Training

Welcome to the training section. Here you will find everything you need to start training your puppy the basic commands. This includes the Sit, Down and Stand – also you will see how to practise the Recall, Stay and Leave. Walking on the lead will be covered including introducing a collar and lead to your puppy.

When you are training your puppy, there are a few guidelines that will apply to every aspect of training that you should be aware of. Below I have listed them in your training guide, which you should refer to and apply to each training exercise that you practise. You can follow all of the instructions within this book but if you don't use the training guide, then you probably won't make much progress.

TRAINING GUIDE

Timing

Always reward your puppy at the right time. You only have one second to clearly communicate your praise, so don't waste time in offering your treat. You need to have it ready so you can reward the instant your puppy does the right thing. If you have to fumble in a bag or your pocket for the treats, the chances are you will be rewarding something else by the time your puppy gets it.

Reinforce your command

You should *never* allow your puppy to ignore your command. If you ask your puppy to 'sit', then you must make sure he does it for you. One of the most common problems with dogs over the age of six months is that they ignore their owners. Dogs will only learn to ignore you if you allow them to. With this in mind, it is far better for you to give only a few commands a day which you ensure your puppy responds to, rather than give 20, most of which will be ignored. You must teach your puppy that you mean what you say, so don't ask your puppy to do something if you don't have time to stop and reinforce your request.

Don't tell your puppy off

If you are faced with your puppy ignoring you, then you need to decide whether he is actually ignoring you, or whether it is that he isn't clear about what you mean. If a dog doesn't understand what you are saying, generally he will do nothing. Remember to keep training simple, and the words you use while training should be used by everyone involved with your puppy to avoid confusion. If necessary, take a step back in your training to ensure your puppy does understand you. If your puppy really is ignoring you, then stay calm, get your puppy's attention and reinforce your command. Use leads where necessary.

Practise

You need to practise little and often with your training. By working with your puppy, reinforcing your training every day, you will be forming the habits that are the good behaviour you are looking for. The methods in this book use 'reward-based training'. This principle uses positive reinforcement by rewarding your puppy for the 'right' behaviour. This will over the long term, shape them into the happy, well adjusted adult dog you are looking for. Always praise your puppy for looking at you. The best habit you can create is getting your puppy to look at you. When he regularly 'checks in' with you, you will find you have much more control, because you won't be struggling to get his attention all the time.

Distractions

A large proportion of owners report that their dog is 'really good indoors', but when they go outside they 'run off and completely ignore them'. Often, owners do not concentrate on training in different environments which leads to the problems of dogs being easily distracted when outside. Try and practise all the training you do, everywhere you go. When you teach your puppy to sit, teach him first at home, and then in the garden, on the pavement, in the park and when up close to another dog. Start easy and build up to training against the hardest distractions. Do the same for all areas of your training and you will find that your puppy will grow up to listen to you everywhere you go, rather than just in the front room or the training hall.

6

Walking on the Lead

INTRODUCING A COLLAR AND LEAD

You can introduce a collar and lead almost immediately to your puppy. It is far better to get him used to wearing a collar and lead in and around the home before you start taking him out with it on. This way, he will be comfortable wearing them before having to deal with being outside in the big wide world.

Introducing the collar

♦ Introduce the collar first, you can put it on at a time when your puppy will be distracted. Maybe when he is going to have his dinner or when you are going to have a play session with him.

◆ Check the collar fits properly, you should be able to fit 1 or 2 fingers underneath. However, ensure the collar is not too loose otherwise your puppy could slip out of it while you are out walking.

◆ If your puppy scratches or rolls around trying to remove the collar, try to distract him by offering toys or playing with him. A collar will not hurt your puppy and he will simply need a little time getting used to the feel of it around his neck. If you keep removing the collar he may learn that if he makes enough fuss, you will take it off. Put the collar on and leave it on.

Introducing the lead

◆ When your puppy is used to wearing his collar, you can introduce him to his lead. Start by clipping the lead on and just walking in and around your home. Encourage him to follow you and praise him for doing so.

◆ Don't drag your puppy along. He may be wary of the lead at first and while he gets used to it, you should be luring him to walk with you rather than dragging him along the floor.

◆ Don't treat the lead as a toy and don't leave it lying around for your puppy to play with or chew up. If he wants to play with it, distract him with something more exciting.

THE TYPE OF COLLAR AND LEAD TO CHOOSE

There are many collars and leads on the market. You will need to get your puppy a soft and lightweight set to begin with. Don't spend too much, he will grow out of it quickly and before you know it you will be purchasing another! Look for a soft weave nylon that you can pierce with the buckle to get it at just the right size for your puppy.

When he gets a little bigger, even if it still fits, you may find the small collar and lead is not very useful, particularly if you have a medium – large size breed.

Choosing the collar

When choosing your next collar I would generally advise using a nylon type. These are easy to clean and put in the wash if necessary. I do like quality leather collars as well, but they struggle if you have a dog who likes getting wet or who thoroughly enjoys rolling in unmentionables! (Like mine.) Try and purchase good quality nylon, as I have met a few dogs with a feint coloured tinge around their neck where the colour has run. As for the rest, we don't use check (choke) chains in training nowadays and some of the plastic/cheap leather collars can be quite stiff and their lack of flexibility can make them rub and uncomfortable to wear.

Choosing the lead

Basically, look for a lead of decent length to help you with training. You will see as you read on that you should use a lead to help you train and not just to hang on to your dog! Many pet shops sell leads that are not suitable for training. They may have lots of different colours and pretty designs but often they are too short and again, too stiff and inflexible for training purposes.

What is more important than the type of lead is the length. My advice is to purchase a lead that is 6' long if you have a small or medium breed or at least 5' long if you have a large breed. Any one of the following will be suitable.

Leather leads

Quality leather (I use Bridle leather) are often the best to help with boisterous bigger breeds. They don't burn or cut into your hands and are easy to grip without your hands slipping.

Nylon leads

These are suitable if your dog is not pulling too much because they are easy to clean. They can cut into your hand though if your dog is too boisterous and you need to hold on to your lead.

Nylon/cotton padded leads

These are a good middle of the range lead. They are reasonably priced and easy to clean. The fact they are padded prevents them cutting into your hand to the extent a normal nylon lead would.

TIP

Leads to avoid are chain leads which are totally impractical for training: they can be dangerous if they are swinging around and will hurt your hand like no other you will come across!

STARTING TO WALK YOUR PUPPY ON THE LEAD

You can start walking your puppy in and around the home once he has been with you a week or so and has settled in! When your puppy has had his vaccinations and is allowed out, then you may begin walking him outside.

HOW TO START

Remember to relax. Don't make a big issue about walking. Your puppy will have a lot to take in when you start walking outside. Hopefully, you will already have introduced the collar and lead so your puppy will feel confident wearing them.

Start taking your puppy outside in short bursts. Ideally, go outside and just 'hang around'. Some new owners start marching up the High Street with their puppy in tow, but he will need to look around and take things in, so allow some time for this. You may find you have no choice anyway because often puppies will sit down and refuse to walk anywhere! Be patient and build up walking slowly. Stay relaxed and keep your lead as loose as possible. Don't encourage your puppy to worry about his environment by keep picking him up, or holding your lead so tightly that you are practically strangling him!

HOW FAR TO WALK

Hopefully when you bought your puppy your breeder will have given you guidelines regarding activity levels. Your puppy is growing until the age of one so it is not wise to over exercise him. Too much running around, long walks and boisterous play can damage his growing bones so be careful to restrict him if necessary. Start walking in short bursts, 10-15 minutes, especially while he is getting used to being outside anyway. As he gets older, you can allow him some more, but be sensible, a 20 minute walk on the lead isn't the same as a 20 minute romp around the fields!

I have met puppies who are finding their walks too tiring and they will often just stop on the walk. You may even notice limps or stiffness caused by aching joints. I once met a puppy who would limp every Monday at Training Classes and when I pointed it out the owner said she was usually fine all week. I later found out that she used to spend all day Sunday romping around with another dog in the family! Often puppies don't know when to stop – make the decision for them!

THE CORRECT WAY TO WALK YOUR PUPPY ON THE LEAD

When walking on the lead you need to enforce a few rules. If you don't, your puppy will make rules of his own and trust me, you won't like them much!

While you are walking your puppy, who is soon to be an adult dog, you need to be in control. You will not be in control if you own a dog who chooses to do what he likes during the walk.

If you lack authority on the end of the lead, your puppy will have no confidence in you as their leader. Therefore, as they grow older, they may take it upon themselves to deal with situations themselves, rather than depend on you. A good example of this is a dog who is nervous of other dogs. As he sees one approach, he starts barking and snarling at it. He has no confidence in his owner because his owner has never really done much and usually just follows him around, so he decides to look after himself. A strong and confident leader would not allow their dog to get into this frame of mind in the first place!

WALKING RULES

1. Keep your puppy on one side only. Most dogs are trained to walk on the left. If you are right handed this usually works well, if you are left handed, the right side may suit you better. *Do not* allow your dog to cross over you, either in front or behind.

2. Do not allow your puppy to stop and sniff or wee on whatever they choose. You must keep moving and stay in control of the walk. If you allow your puppy to cross over you to sniff this tree and then wee on that lamppost, he is dictating the walk. Not only do you have no control over him, but it is also dangerous while he weaves in and around everyone's legs!

3. Praise your puppy every time he looks up at you or is walking next to you on a loose lead (not pulling). You need to reinforce his good behaviour. If you don't tell your puppy what you like, then he won't know. The more praise and reward you give when he is doing the right thing, the more he will do it, thus creating the good habit of 'walking to heel'. Please watch your timing, ONLY praise if your puppy is looking at you or not pulling on the lead.

STOPPING YOUR PUPPY PULLING ON THE LEAD

This is actually quite simple. Do not allow him to get away with it. If your puppy keeps pulling out ahead of you, then you must give a consequence to his action. You can practise the techniques below.

1. Look at the walking rules. Are you following them? If you are allowing your puppy to stop and sniff at what he likes on the walk, then it is only natural that in his excitement he will pull you to get on to the next fabulous smell.

2. Try just stopping. Don't allow him to get distracted and start sniffing around the area, but wait until the lead goes loose, praise and begin on your walk again.

3. Try changing direction. This is very effective. If your puppy pulls out ahead of you, then stop and go the other way. You definitely need a long lead for this exercise to succeed: allow your puppy to pull as far away as possible from you before you turn and go the other way. This exercise serves a number of purposes and is my favourite for getting results.

   a) Changing direction when your puppy pulls teaches him that if he feels the lead pull tight, there is a consequence. He doesn't get to where he is pulling to, but quite the opposite!

   b) Many owners lack control because they are unable to get their dogs' attention. By changing direction, instead of you following your puppy, he now has to follow you. You will get the opportunity to praise him when he looks at you (to see where you are going) and praise him when the lead goes loose as he walks towards you.

   c) It will make your puppy aware that there is someone at the end of the lead. If you have a puppy who couldn't care less who's trotting along behind them then this is a great exercise. Until your puppy will look to you of his own accord, you need to make him do so by manipulating the situation.

HARNESSES AND NORMAL COLLARS

I recommend starting with a collar. You can teach your puppy to walk with you without pulling, you just need to invest a little time and effort while he is young. In fact, I am not a lover of harnesses at all. I often ask owners why they have chosen to walk their dog on a harness and the most common answer is that they feel they have more control. The second most popular answer is that they don't want to use a collar because their dog pulls so much that it makes them cough and wheeze. Personally, I think that with regards to control, it is not that owners actually *do* have more control, more that they feel they have 'hold' of their dog. With regards to the pressure on the neck, well undoubtedly this does cause some dogs to cough and wheeze, although if you train them to walk with you well, it wouldn't be a problem at all.

My dislike of harnesses is because most of them are ineffective in *helping* with your training. Those which just wrap around your dog seem to encourage them to pull all the more. Like a husky or any animal who is pulling something, a harness gets strapped around them so they can spread their weight, lean into the harness and pull. Other dogs simply like the feel of being encased in a harness, I often see them leaning into the harness, normally away from their owner and the result is the owners are still being pulled but out to the side instead.

Often when we remove the harness from these dogs, they usually walk much better on their collar and their owners are amazed at the improvement. There are only a couple of harnesses on the market I would use, and these only because it really is necessary. As your dog gets older if you feel you may want to use a harness, speak to a trainer as they can advise you on the most effective products and other options available, such as headcollars, which may be better to help you with training.

COMMON PROBLEMS AND SOLUTIONS TO WALKING YOUR DOG ON A LEAD

My puppy keeps chewing the lead

♦ Watching a lead waving around can be very attractive. Puppies will play with most things while they are young and exploring, but don't allow them to get away with chewing their lead. Until they learn the 'leave' command, you will need to manipulate the situation to avoid them doing this.

♦ Never leave the lead lying around for your puppy to play with indoors.

♦ When walking, don't wave the lead around which could entice your puppy to play with it. Remember to keep the lead loose and relaxed at all times.

♦ Try stopping walking and distracting your puppy. Use a toy, preferably one which makes a noise to help you.

♦ Try spraying the lead with a puppy anti-chew spray. It may discourage him from chewing if it doesn't taste very nice.

My puppy won't walk anywhere

♦ You may be rushing him a little. Remember to introduce him to the big wide world gradually. Go outside and just let him take it all in.

♦ Try taking your puppy to the park, in the car if necessary. You can teach him that going outside is fun and most puppies will enjoy this environment, the space to play and meeting other dogs and people. Don't forget to take a favourite toy to help build his confidence outside.

♦ Remember not to reinforce any fear. Don't praise, treat or cuddle your puppy if he is showing any signs of nervousness. Be confident and in control and concentrate on making it fun to be outside.

My puppy walks but keeps sitting down and refusing to go any further

There may be a couple of reasons for this. You will need to assess the situation and decide which one applies as you will resolve the problems in different ways.

♦ Your puppy may just be too tired. Many owners, without realizing over-exercise their puppies. Generally, this is well intentioned, as owners are trying to give their puppy a good exercise regime, but they can start this too early. If your puppy just sits and has lost interest in the walk and his surroundings, it may be that he is struggling to cope with his levels of exercise.

♦ Your puppy may feel overwhelmed by being outside, particularly if you have taken him to a new environment. Try giving him a minute to take on board the new sights and sounds and then encourage him to walk on with you.

♦ Your puppy may be refusing to walk on because he wants to sniff, or say hello to someone or another dog. When puppies become confident outside, you need to ensure you remain in control. There is a fine line between your puppy getting used to being outside and your puppy starting to dictate the walk. You can tell if this happens, because rather than just sitting down and not moving, your puppy will stop but will be sniffing and distracted or trying to pull you over to what they want to do or see. If this starts to happen, you need to reinforce the walking rules, before you find yourself with no authority at your end of the lead.

My puppy keeps jumping up at me when I walk him on the lead

♦ Don't encourage him to jump up at all – check Chapter 4 on jumping up and make sure that at all times, your puppy is taught that jumping up is not acceptable.

♦ Don't wave the lead around. This may encourage your puppy to get excited and start jumping about to play.

♦ If you are carrying treats or using them to lure your puppy, don't hold them too high in your hand. It will encourage your puppy to jump and try and get to them. It is better to keep treats in an 'easy to access' pouch for when you need them.

♦ If your puppy is actually jumping: stop walking, stand still and upright, keep the lead loose and relaxed and turn away. If necessary, hold the lead away from you to keep your puppy from reaching you when jumping. Don't move on until your puppy has completely stopped jumping and is calm.

My puppy keeps picking things up off the ground and trying to eat them

This is a very common problem. Until your puppy has learnt the 'leave' command and will do so when you ask, you will need to be very vigilant.

♦ Be very aware of your surroundings. Try to avoid going too close to temptation and if your puppy tries to pick something up, speed up and say the word 'leave' as you walk past. Make sure your puppy does not get the opportunity to pick it up.

♦ Carry some nice treats with you – if your puppy does manage to pick something up, hold out a treat in the palm of your hand to offer in exchange. As your puppy *opens* his mouth to drop the item, say 'leave' and reward with your treat.

♦ Try carrying a squeaky toy and use it to distract your puppy away from items on the floor – don't forget to praise him when you get his attention.

7

Sit, Down and Stand

WHY SHOULD I TEACH MY PUPPY THESE POSITIONS?

It is extremely useful to teach your puppy these basic positions.
You can use them to communicate and help you keep control
in many situations. Often, using commands that your puppy
understands well can be reassuring and calming at times when
he may be feeling nervous or getting too excited. We teach three
positions because when many people practise, they often only
use the sit and down. The problem with this is that many dogs
will learn what is coming next and so will anticipate your next
command. When you say 'sit' he does, but will then dive straight
into a down, without you even asking. I see this anticipation
in many situations with owners and their dogs and it is a good

example of how dogs will learn a routine and then guess what is coming next.

The problem, then, is that your puppy is making decisions of his own when actually the aim is to train him to be listening to you. The least used of these positions in everyday life will be the stand, although it is useful for you to know how to achieve the stand for occasions, such as a visit to the vet. The sit and down will be used frequently everyday and you will find having this element of control will prove invaluable.

LEARNING TO SIT

1. Hold a treat in your hand.

2. Show your puppy the treat by placing it right in front of his nose.

3. Slowly move the treat away from you, over his head, so that his nose follows the treat and points upwards.

4. As his head looks up to follow the treat his bottom should go down into a sit position.

5. Feed him the treat and say the word 'sit' at the same time.

COMMON PROBLEMS AND SOLUTIONS TO LEARNING TO SIT

I have tried to get my puppy to sit but he doesn't do it

♦ You may be moving the treat too quickly.

♦ Your treat may not be tasty enough to hold his interest and follow it with his nose.

♦ If he is jumping, you are holding the treat too high – try holding it a little lower.

♦ If he is eating the treat before sitting, you may be holding it too close to his nose or moving it upwards too slowly.

My puppy will sit for a treat but ignores me otherwise

The point of using treats is to reward your puppy when he gets it right. After a while, he will know what you want him to do when you say 'sit'. At this point, you should reduce the amount of treats he has. Make sure that when you practise any new exercise you use treats to train it, and then reduce the quantity of treats that you offer. Perhaps do so for every third sit, or if he does it really well. Don't let your puppy get into the habit of receiving food *all* the time. Remember that toys and praise should also be used as rewards.

My puppy will sit indoors but not outside

♦ This is usually a case of puppies not being trained outside. There are many distractions outside and you should be practising training your puppy around them.

♦ Being outside is often more exciting than being at home, so take more interesting treats than those you use indoors, which will help you gain *and* keep your puppy's attention.

♦ Make sure that you reinforce your command and don't let your puppy get away with ignoring you. Do not move on until he has sat, and this will teach him that you will be patient and will always wait until he does it.

♦ Try practising where there are not many distractions and then get closer to other people and dogs and try getting your puppy to sit when up close to them.

My puppy will sit for the treat but gets up immediately and wanders off

♦ Make sure you keep your puppy in the sit before you allow him to get up again.

♦ This is a very common problem and easily resolved.

—When your puppy sits, keep the treat in your fingers for a few seconds before he is allowed to eat it.

—Check your timing, if your puppy is not in the sit *when* you feed the treat then your timing is not right. If he stands up when you offer the treat, make him sit again before you give it to him.

My puppy will sit when I say but not when others in the family ask him to

♦ This is generally because other family members have not practised with your puppy or they are not firm enough when asking him to sit.

♦ Show them how to do it properly and remember not to override any other family member. If someone has asked your puppy to sit, let them persevere until they achieve it. If you override their command, remember how it affects your hierarchy: it can lead your puppy to think that other family members are not very important and that he doesn't have to listen to them.

LEARNING TO DOWN

Before you start teaching the down, make sure your puppy has a good 'sit'. He should be able to sit for a few seconds and if he is not at this stage yet, practise a little more before you begin.

1. Start by telling your puppy to sit. He should be sitting in front of you.

2. Hold your treat in front of your puppy's nose so he is aware you have it.

3. Slowly pull the treat down towards the floor, just in front of his paws.

4. As his head and shoulders follows your treat down to the floor, keep hold of the treat, keep your hand still and wait. Your puppy should completely lie down as he tries to reach for the treat in your hand. Be patient.

5. As soon as your puppy does lie down, say 'down' and release the treat.

COMMON PROBLEMS AND SOLUTIONS TO LEARNING TO 'DOWN'

I have tried to lure my puppy down but he just sits still or gets up

♦   If your puppy sits still and doesn't follow the treat with his nose, then you probably need to try tastier treats.

♦   You may find him more interested in following the food if you practise when he is hungry.

♦   You may be moving the treat too quickly, try doing it more slowly next time.

♦   If your puppy stands up, then you need to put him back in the sit and try again. You may need to practise your sit a little more: remember that he needs to be able to sit for a few seconds because if he doesn't, you won't have a good starting position to lure him into the down.

My puppy seems to get bored and loses interest when I try to get him 'down'

♦ Try using tastier treats which will keep his interest.

♦ Try practising in an area where there are less distractions while he learns.

♦ While your puppy is young, try to keep training sessions short and successful.

My puppy crawls/walks forward or stands up to get to the treat

♦ If your puppy crawls forward to get the treat, then you are holding it too far away from him. Remember that when you pull the treat down to the floor, you must keep it still, just in front of his paws.

♦ If your puppy stands up then:

—You may be moving the treat downwards too quickly.
—You may be pulling the treat out or along the floor away from your puppy rather than downwards in front of him.

My puppy keeps jumping around or using his paws to try and get the treat

♦ If your puppy is behaving like this he may be too excited by the treat you are using. You may need to use a less appetising treat, such as his normal dried food. He could also be too hungry which is causing him to get so excited.

♦ If your puppy behaves like this, put him back in the sit and start again. Make sure that your puppy doesn't get the treat as a result of this bouncy behaviour. If his excitement seems impossible to stop, try again later when he is more calm.

My puppy will lay down when following the treat but not if I just say 'down'

♦ You are using the treat to lure your puppy into a position. When he does what you want, you reward him with the treat and say the word which you want your puppy to associate with that position. While your puppy is learning, you will need to repeat the exercise over and over until he has heard 'down' enough times to associate it with that position. Some puppies can get this in a matter of days, others can take a number of weeks. However, the speed at which he will learn, often depends on how good your timing is and how often you practise.

♦ If, after a number of weeks, your puppy will not lay down when you say, you may have been using your command at the wrong time. A common mistake is that owners, knowing what they want their puppy to do, forget that their puppy does not yet know what the word means. This means owners will say 'down' when they are trying to lure their puppy into this position, instead of waiting until their puppy is actually in the 'down', before putting the word to the action. Practise using your command at exactly the right time and you should see your puppy beginning to understand you.

♦ Another cause of this problem is that you have over-used the treats and your puppy just won't do it if there isn't a treat waiting for him. When your puppy goes easily into the down, you should stop treating him every time and only reward intermittently, using praise and fuss as a reward sometimes, instead of food. Once your puppy has heard the 'down' enough to understand it's meaning, you should be able to say 'down' and he should do it for you, without you having to be on your hands and knees in front of him.

My puppy has started barking at me to get the treat

♦ This is caused by one of two things. Either
    1. Your puppy has learned previously that barking at you gets him what he wants, and so is going to try and get the same result here.
    2. Your puppy is frustrated and doesn't know what to do to get the treat.

♦ Either way, never reward a puppy for barking at you and you should stand up, turn your back on him, break all eye contact and walk away. Return after a few moments and try again. Your reaction will be effective in teaching your puppy:

    —If he barks at you to get what he wants, the result is that he will get nothing, not even your attention.
    —If he barks at you because he is frustrated and doesn't know what to do, you have successfully communicated that barking isn't what you were after – try something else.

LEARNING TO STAND

Again, with this position you should start with a relatively good sit. Your puppy should be sitting in front of you before you begin.

1. Hold your treat right in front of your puppy's nose.

2. Pull the treat slowly away from your puppy so that he reaches forward to follow it.

3. As you lure him forward, he should pull himself up into a stand.

4. Feed him the treat and say 'stand'.

COMMON PROBLEMS AND SOLUTIONS TO LEARNING TO STAND

My puppy just sits there and doesn't follow the treat to stand up

♦ You may be moving the treat away too quickly. Your puppy will not follow it forwards if it goes out of his reach too quickly.

♦ As your puppy leans forward, encourage him with a little praise. You can also take a step backwards yourself which will make him more likely to stand up to follow you.

My puppy jumps up to try and get the treat

◆ You are probably holding your treat too high. It needs to be at nose level, any higher and he may be tempted to jump and try and get it.

◆ If you are in the habit of snatching treats or food away from your puppy, then he may just be trying to grab the treat before you do this again.

My puppy gets up and I feed him the treat but he immediately sits back down again

◆ Don't feed your treat too quickly. Hold onto it for a few seconds while he remains in the stand.

◆ You may also find it beneficial to hold the treat slightly lower than his nose, *once* he is up in the stand. This is because if your puppy's head is lowered a little, he won't lower his rear end at the same time.

8

Recall

When asked, the recall, is one of the most common problems owners tend to have with their puppies. I will detail here how to train the recall in a step-by-step guide. Be warned, if you move onto the next step too early, or do not correct your puppy as detailed, then you will risk having problems with your recall.

If your puppy will not come back to you when you call him, then you should not be letting him off the lead. Likewise, if your puppy chases off across the park, leaving you spluttering in a cloud of dust, then again, you should not be letting him off the lead.

Your puppy is your responsibility and if you do not have control when he is off the lead then do not allow him to carry on and 'do his own thing'. This can lead to real problems as your puppy gets older and has got into the bad habit of running off and ignoring your every command.

WHAT YOU NEED

♦ **A long line** I tend to use tracking leads rather than the extendable flexi-leads. I find that for training recalls they are much more useful and in this chapter you will learn how to use them.

♦ **A couple of toys** Use toys which your dog likes the best. Does he prefer balls or frisbees? What about ragger (tug) toys? You should experiment with toys and find which ones your dog *loves*. Whichever you choose, you should keep these toys to be played with only when you are out walking. Never let your dog play with them at any other time and don't leave them lying around your house.

♦ **A treat box** Use a plastic box or small tin with treats in that will make a noise when shaken.

♦ **Treats** You should take with you three to four different varieties.

TREATS AND REWARDS

Reward doesn't necessarily mean treat. It can also mean play or attention. Many owners make the mistake of giving freely the things that they should make their dogs works for. This can result in your dog taking it all for granted which will leave you trying desperately to get his attention but finding he is not interested in anything you have to offer.

Treats

When training outside, you should never use the same treats you would use at home. Remember, when outside, your distractions are far greater and there are many more interesting things to grab your puppy's attention. If you use different treats, after a short while, your puppy will realize this and is likely to be far more interested in them, knowing that this will be his only opportunity to get them today. You will need a selection of these 'special' treats and you should ensure they are ones that will appeal to your puppy. I would take three types of treat with me and I would offer the one which best suited my puppy's behaviour. For example:

♦ Puppy comes back when called but there are no other distractions around.
  Offer a small meaty dog treat.

♦ Puppy comes back when called and he chose to do this rather than run across the park to the kids playing with a football, despite the fact that he saw them and he loves footballs.
  Offer a tastier dog treat – normally liver.

♦ Puppy comes back when called even though he was playing with another dog or getting stroked/attention from somebody else.
  Offer a fresh meat treat, such as chicken or sausage.

I hope you can see the point. Make sure your treat rewards the behaviour – if your puppy does something really well, reward him with a treat that acknowledges this.

Toys

As already mentioned, you should reserve your puppy's most favourite toys for when you really need them (when in the park). Too much of something makes it boring, but restricting access to valued toys means your puppy will be much more likely to be interested when you offer them.

With regard to using the toys, many dogs will lose interest (except Border Collies, I concede) even in their favourite toys when faced with exciting distractions outside. You can keep your puppy toy motivated, as long as you use toys to gain your dog's attention, rather than just to kick around the park.

♦   As mentioned previously, experiment with toys and find out which ones your puppy really likes. Keep a couple of these toys aside for taking out with you – but don't get every one out each time you are on a walk.

♦   When you have your dog's attention, start playing with the toy. Only play for a couple of minutes each time and *before* your puppy loses interest you should put the toy away. In order to keep him interested and motivated in your toys, you need to keep in control of them. Always play like this with toys when you are out, which will teach your puppy that if he wants to play with you and the toy, he had better take the opportunity when it is offered.

♦ Now practise gaining your dog's attention with a toy. Without distractions around, when your puppy looks at you, whip out your toy and start to play with it. Call your puppy and as he runs over to join in, praise and throw/play with the toy with him. Make it fun and don't become boring by making him sit when he gets there. Keep practising and try this technique against distractions (remembering to start easy and build up to more difficult distractions).

RECALL TRAINING GUIDE

1. Teach your puppy what 'come' means. At home and in the garden, practise calling your puppy and every time he runs to you, praise him by saying 'Good Boy to Come'. While beginning training, only ever use the word 'come' if your puppy is running towards you. This will teach him that 'come' means to run to you, because your timing is good as you are putting your command to the action. After a short while, he will have a good understanding of the command and should know what you want when you call it.

2. Take your puppy outside and begin training in the park. You can leave a tracking line attached to his collar so that he will have some freedom and can get a distance from you. When you want to call him, clearly shout his name and 'come'. Remember to use a happy, enticing voice and open body language. As he runs towards you, praise him and you can then reward him when he gets there.

   When your puppy is reliable and will come when there are no distractions around, you should try and get him to come when there are. Start with simple things, such as calling him while he is sniffing around or if he is looking (focusing) at something in the distance. If he comes back, praise and reward him with a treat. If you call and he makes no move to 'come', use the lead to pull him in, thus teaching him that when you call, even if he is concentrating on something else, he still has to listen and come. Build up to practising against harder distractions such as greeting another dog or getting attention from another person.

3. When walking in the park, don't walk the same route around the edges of the park everyday. Owners whose dogs run off, have dogs who are too secure in their environment and often know that their owners will be waiting at the gate for them when they decide they are ready to go home. You must constantly change direction, and if you are using a tracking lead you can still do this. *Don't call your puppy*, just simply turn and walk in the opposite direction. Keep doing this all the time on your walk. This will mean that your puppy will be following you instead of the other way around. If your puppy runs up to you while you do this, simply praise and reward, saying 'Good boy to come'. What you are doing, is creating the habit of getting your puppy to watch out for you, because he will never know where you are going to be next. In the long term, this will give you a dog who you will rarely even have to call, because he is already regularly 'checking in' with you to see where you are going now. This is the insecurity you need to create to avoid your dog running off or ignoring you in the park.

4. Using a tracking line will help teach your puppy your boundaries. It will keep him close to you and over a period of time, he will learn that he should be keeping within this

distance from you. When you reach another dog, if your puppy likes to play then let him play. You can let him off the lead to play if the other owner isn't going to walk off in the opposite direction, with your puppy in tow. This will teach your puppy that he can play with others and have good fun but he is not allowed to go rushing off across the park to get to them. When you need to finish the play, use your treat box to rattle and encourage your puppy back over to you. Reward him for coming and put the lead back on before moving on.

5. When you feel your puppy has made good progress – is regularly looking for you and coming back when you call – you can try to move on to the next step by dropping the tracking line. This is why these leads are so useful. You can let your puppy trail the lead, so you are testing his reliability off lead while having some security for yourself, that if he were to try and run off, you have a long lead you can grab, or stamp your foot on, to get him back. Likewise, if he does run away from you, he has a lead attached, so that when you reach him, you can simply pick it up and correct him – this is far easier and calmer than chasing around, trying to catch a puppy who is having a whale of a time avoiding you. When your puppy is reliable at this stage, you can then get rid of the lead altogether.

Remember not to rush your recall training. It will only take a few occasions of your puppy running off and ignoring you, before he thinks he can do it all of the time. Sometimes it can be easier to build up his reliability in the park at quieter times of the day. At 8am, the parks can be packed out with owners walking their dogs before work. If your puppy finds it all *too* distracting and overexciting, try walking at a quieter time for a while to help you succeed in gaining his attention yourself. The more success you have, the more you can praise and reward. The more you can praise and reward, the more your puppy will adopt the behaviours you are looking for.

COMMON PROBLEMS AND SOLUTIONS WHEN LEARNING RECALL

My puppy is ignoring my recall

◆ If your puppy is off the lead, you should put him back on. If your puppy is ignoring your recall, you have no control and you need to practise reinforcing your training.

◆ Practise recalls on the lead as mentioned in the recall training guide.

My puppy keeps running off

◆ If your puppy keeps running off, you must keep him on a lead. Often, puppies see things, such as other dogs across the park, and become so excited, they run full speed ahead to get there and play.

◆ You need to teach your puppy that he can play, but not until you get there. Use your lead to reinforce the boundaries you want to enforce.

My puppy isn't interested in treats when outside the house

◆ This is because life outside the house is much more exciting. Therefore, your treats need to be much more exciting too. You should always use different treats outside to those you use at home. This will make them much more interesting. For example, if you are feeding dried complete food at home, try using fresh meat as your treat outside. A puppy who doesn't get fresh meat at home, will often be interested when you offer some chicken or sausage when you are out on a walk!

♦ Also, you can try training with your puppy outside when he is hungry. Instead of feeding breakfast before your walk, try feeding it afterwards instead (remember, you should wait one hour before feeding after exercise). Or you could even take his breakfast with you to use as treats on the walk instead. Either way, the hungrier he is, the more interested in your treats he will be.

When should I let my puppy off the lead completely?

♦ You will have to use your judgement here. Basically if your puppy will not come when you call him or goes running off a long way from you then you should not be letting him off the lead. As a general rule, the earlier you let your puppy off the lead, the more success you can have with keeping him with you. The reason for this is that when a puppy is very young, he will find the outside world, particularly big, open spaces quite daunting and will often feel insecure. This insecurity is what makes your puppy want to stay near you. As they get older, say five to six months onwards, your puppy becomes confident in these environments: having been there lots of times now and knowing that you are always there when he wants you. This is the age that if you let him off the lead for the first time, he is likely to be overwhelmed with excitement and disappear for fun and frolics once he has realized he is free.

◆ Many owners will be lulled into a false sense of security as their young puppy is 'good as gold' but suddenly find that as they get older, they start running off and ignoring them. This could often be prevented if owners work with their puppy and practise recall training from the very first day, before they get to the point where they are experiencing problems.

Although my puppy runs off, if I don't let him off the lead to run around, he won't wear himself out or get enough exercise
I hear this comment all the time. Another one is that owners feel 'mean' or 'guilty' if they don't let them off to have fun, run around and be a dog.

Well, what's worse? That you keep your dog on a lead or the following happens?

◆ Your puppy runs around the park, jumping on people and other dogs, upsetting many owners and their dogs. What about the small children who it would frighten to have a puppy jumping all over them, or the older people who can easily be knocked over by a reasonably sized dog running at full speed towards them?

◆ Your puppy runs out of the park into the road, cars swerving to avoid him, although many do not manage to, and there are sadly numerous dogs who have lost their lives in this way.

◆ Your puppy gets himself into trouble, charging towards and jumping all over an older dog who has no patience due to the pain of the arthritis in his back legs. He receives a small but painful bite for his efforts which may develop into a behaviour problem for your puppy, who now associates this breed or all dogs as aggressive and decides to nip them first before they nip him.

♦ Your puppy beats you to the broken beer bottles and fried chicken bones that users of the park dumped in there the previous night. You are too late to stop him crunching up the chicken bones which may splinter in his stomach and you may need a traumatic (for you both) visit to the vet which could easily have been avoided.

♦ You are late back for work because this lunchtime, your puppy has decided that he won't come back to you but will spend half an hour running here, there and everywhere while you stand at the gate calling, calling and calling him while getting very stressed and angry.

Now we have looked at the possibilities of letting a dog you have no control over off the lead, we can look at the actual argument.

♦ You can easily give your dog enough exercise. Using a tracking line gives them the freedom to run around, and is ideal for playing with you, with toys or for meeting other dogs. Exercise doesn't have to be continuous running, in fact most dogs spend most of their walk trotting around the park. Fast walking on the lead and the opportunity to play will be enough. If you are practising training in the park as you should be, this can be pretty tiring for a puppy – in fact, training is often a great source of using up energy.

♦ As for feeling guilty – forget it! If you have guilty feelings over this then there is something wrong with your ideas on dog ownership. Go back and read the chapter on pack hierarchy. Remember, your puppy is your responsibility and feeling bad about not letting them off the lead should never override your responsibilities to avoid the scenarios above becoming a part of your life.

Should I praise my puppy for coming back to me, even though he has spent the last half an hour running round the park and not coming when I called him?

This is an interesting one, as there are generally two sides of this argument. Some say that you should reward your puppy for coming back, even though you have been led a merry dance for the last half an hour. Others say that you shouldn't because he didn't come back when you called.

I would tend to favour the latter but be sensible regarding the time involved.

♦ If your puppy ignores a couple of your recalls but does respond after this and so comes relatively quickly, i.e. within a minute or so, then I would treat and praise, especially if he has left play or attention to come back to you.

♦ If you spend any longer than this trying to recall your puppy back to you and they come eventually, then I would just put them on the lead, not say anything and offer no reward. This means you are not telling them off for coming back but you are also not rewarding the fact that they have ignored you.

Should I tell my puppy off for not coming back to me?

♦ No, it is unlikely that you will get your timing good enough for your puppy to associate your reprimand with the fact that they didn't come back when called. It is far better to work with positive training methods than negative ones to get a better long term result and to avoid damaging your relationship with your puppy.

♦ When working with adult dogs, we may use different techniques, but remember that your puppy is only learning at this stage, so you need to keep calm and firmly teach him right from wrong by sticking to a consistent training programme.

I had to go and get my puppy because he ignored my recall, I put him on the lead to punish him and after a few minutes let him off again. Is this right?

♦ Generally, no. I often see this in the park and the long-term result is that these actions on your behalf do not change your puppy's behaviour. The reason is that often, when let back off the lead again, your puppy will continue to ignore your recall the next time. You need to be training as detailed in the training guide (page 123). Often dogs will happily 'suffer' the few minutes on the lead as a result of their behaviour, many probably think it is worth it because chasing off in the park with next door's Labrador was such great fun.

♦ The answer here is – don't let your dog off the lead. If your puppy starts ignoring you like this then put a stop to it, before it becomes a bad habit. Go back to using your lead for a while so you can communicate to your puppy that he will lose his freedom if he behaves like that. Remember, with all dogs, freedom to run around off lead is not their 'right' – they need to earn it.

My puppy comes back when there is nothing else around, but if there is anything else in the park, he completely ignores me
This is the most common problem of all. When training recalls with owners and their dogs, I often find it is not the recall that they are having problems with, it is the fact that they are unable to gain their dog's attention from a distraction, to recall them back in the first place. There is no magic cure here, you need to follow the training guide and you can see now why it is important to get your dog thinking that he needs to watch out for you in the park. That insecurity is invaluable, because if your dog is in the habit of looking for you to check where you are, you will be able to recall him back easily.

Every time my puppy comes back to me I make him sit and then give him a treat. This worked well for a while but now he is starting to ignore me

♦ The trick to having a well trained dog is to keep him guessing. Often people use the same old routines and frankly, dogs become bored with them. When your puppy always knows what is coming next, it puts him in a position where he can choose whether to do it or not. If your puppy is ignoring your recall because of this, it is likely that you need to change what you are doing.

♦ I always teach owners to get their puppy to sit when they run up to them. It is a useful exercise in practising slowing your puppy down so they don't run into you at high speed. This should hopefully teach them that they don't run and crash into other people as well. However, I always recommend that although you should practise this, remember that variety is the spice of life and when you recall your dog back, always change what you do when he gets there.

—Give him a treat and send him away again.
—Get out a toy and throw it for him.
—Make him sit or lay down.
—Put on his lead and walk with him for a while.
—Lay out a treat trail on the floor – continue walking while dropping a small line of treats for him to follow behind you – send him away again.
—Give him a stroke and fuss and send him away again.

I have been told not to let my dog off the lead until he is six months old, is this right?

♦ There is no right or wrong age to begin letting your puppy off the lead. As mentioned previously, often the earlier the better so you can begin training, and if you wait until six months and just let him off the lead then it is likely that he will just run off enjoying his freedom.

♦ All puppies and their owners are different. Follow the training guide and build up your puppy's reliability with recall practise.

My puppy will come back when my son calls him but completely ignores the rest of us
This is a surprisingly common problem and I think it has more to do with the fact that puppies often see children as fun and more of a playmate than you are.

Have a look at what your puppy does when he runs back to your son and, watch what your son does. The chances are it is very different and more exciting than your own behaviour. Try sticking with the programme and remember, if your puppy is ignoring your recall completely then he shouldn't be off the lead yet.

In the local park where we usually go, my puppy comes back practically every time I call him. We went to a new place today and he completely ignored me

♦ This situation is a good example of the need for owners to take their puppies to lots of different environments and train them everywhere they go. While dogs are young, you need to teach them that the rules remain in force in all environments and working on this through their first year will be invaluable training for as they grow older.

♦ My biggest piece of advice here is when you go to a new place, keep your puppy on the lead. He will experience a rush of adrenaline at the excitement of being somewhere new. If you let him off the lead immediately when you arrive the chances are he will ignore you and run off to investigate his new surroundings. If you wait 10 to 15 minutes before you let him off the lead, the adrenaline rush will have died off and he will be much calmer and more likely to respond to you.

9

Leave and Stay

LEAVE

Teaching your puppy the 'leave' command is extremely useful. It can be adapted to many situations and, if you teach it well, it will help you gain control at those times you really need it.

Start teaching this exercise at home and when your puppy has a good understanding of the 'leave' you can begin to use it in other situations, i.e. when your puppy is picking up things he shouldn't or when you want him to walk past a distraction in the street.

Learning to leave

1. Start by putting your puppy on a lead.

2. Using a treat, place the treat on the floor just out of reach in front of him.

3. As your puppy reaches forward to try and reach the treat, hold onto his lead and firmly say 'leave' every few seconds.

4. Wait until your puppy stops pulling against the lead and turns to look up at you.

5. At this point, give your puppy permission to go forward and eat the treat.

COMMON PROBLEMS AND SOLUTIONS TO LEARNING TO LEAVE

My puppy loses interest in the treat on the floor

◆ Try using a treat which your puppy has not been given before.

◆ You may have put the treat too far away from him on the floor. Move it a little closer to your puppy, it should be just out of his reach.

◆ Can your puppy see the treat? If it blends into your floor or carpet, try using another treat or practising in a different area.

◆ Practise when he is hungry.

My puppy keeps pulling and pulling and doesn't stop

◆ He will. Make sure you are just holding onto the lead to stop him reaching the treat. If you are pulling him back with the lead, then this may be the cause of the problem. Most puppies stop pulling against the lead relatively quickly, but if your puppy is very focused on the treat and takes a little longer, just be patient. Patience is a great training aid and if you just wait, your puppy will stop pulling.

My puppy stops pulling on the lead but doesn't turn to look at me

◆ This is a common problem. When your puppy is really focused on the treat, he may stop pulling because he has realized he isn't getting anywhere but instead of turning to look at you, he will just stare at the treat. If your puppy does this, simply call his name in a light and 'happy' voice and as he turns to look up at you, give him permission to go and eat the treat.

I give my puppy permission to eat the treat but he doesn't, he just looks at me

♦   This is a case of your puppy not knowing what to do. One minute you are holding him back and the next you are telling him to go and get it. You probably just need to be a little clearer in your instruction. When you give him permission to go and eat the treat, make it clear, perhaps by pointing, taking a step forward yourself and giving permission verbally. I usually say 'Go on' when I want to communicate that it is ok to do something or to signal the finish of an exercise.

Why should I get my puppy to look at me, even though he has 'left' the treat?

♦   This is because it teaches him that it is the 'look' that gets the permission. If your timing is good and you give permission immediately he looks at you, this becomes a good exercise for reinforcing your authority and getting your puppy to look to you for instruction.

Make 'leave' more difficult

When your puppy has mastered this exercise in this simple form, practise making it harder.

1.   Make him sit and 'leave' the treat while you place it on the ground.

2. Try holding his 'look' at you for a few seconds, rather than letting him go and eat the treat immediately.

3. You could place the treat much closer to your puppy and even build up to placing the treats on his paws.

4. Try moving around yourself as he 'leaves' the treat. Often owners practise training while they are standing still and when they start to move, the dog thinks it is signals the end of an exercise, which of course, it shouldn't.

When your puppy has a good understanding of the word 'leave' try applying it to other situations. Try and say 'leave' in the second preceding the event. For example: If your puppy is about to pick up something from the floor – say 'leave' just before he picks it up. Then offer him a toy of his own which he is allowed to have. Maybe if you are out walking and your puppy likes to lunge at people to say 'hello', try saying 'leave' just before he lunges, rather than waiting until he is up on his hind legs licking their face.

If you practise your timing and get it right, you will find the 'leave' more useful in preventing behaviours occur, rather than having to try and recover once they have happened.

Remember to praise and reward when your puppy does it well.

STAY

The stay is another really useful exercise that you can use in many different situations. It is important not to rush any type of training, because you need to make sure that your puppy is reliable with the easy stages before moving onto the harder ones. This is particularly true when teaching the stay. In order to ensure you can achieve a reliable stay with your puppy, don't expect too much too soon or give him the opportunity to keep breaking the stay.

The rules of the stay

1. When you tell your puppy to stay, show him the palm of your hand. This is a clear signal to your puppy that you don't want him to move.

2. When practising, do not hold any treats in your hands. If your puppy sees you holding up a treat, the temptation for him can be so great that he is likely to break the stay to come and get the treat from you. Make sure all treats are out of sight while you practise, maybe keep them in your pocket until you need them.

3. Only use the word 'stay'. If you talk too much you may lose your authority.

4. *Never* call your puppy up out of a stay. This is a very common thing that owners do. If you tell your puppy to stay and then call him to you, he will always be waiting for your call. This means you will not achieve a reliable stay as your puppy will always be anticipating when you will call him. When you practise the stay and you start walking away from your puppy, *always return* to him and release him from the stay.

5. If your puppy keeps breaking the stay, don't persist with it. Make it easier by making it shorter or moving less far away. Having success with this exercise is very important. If you don't achieve the simplest stay, then you won't achieve the harder ones.

Step 1

1. Start by teaching your puppy what 'stay' means. Ask your puppy to sit or lay down (I usually start with the down as most dogs will settle into a stay better in this position).

2. Stand in front of your puppy, hold up the palm of your hand and say 'stay'.

3. After one or two seconds, praise your puppy and finish the exercise.

4. Each day add on another one or two seconds to the time that your puppy remains in the stay.

5. Build up to 15 or 20 seconds while you are standing right in front of your puppy.

Step 2

1. Start with your puppy in the sit or down position.

2. Show your puppy the palm of your hand and say 'stay'.

3. Take a step back away from your puppy. Walk backwards, don't turn your back on him. Wait for one or two seconds and then return to your puppy, remind him to stay as you return. Praise your puppy and finish the exercise.

4. Each day, take another step further away, return to your puppy, praise and finish the exercise.

The next stage

♦ When you can move five to ten paces away from your puppy, try again but instead of returning immediately, build up the time that you wait before going back.

♦ Put your puppy into the 'stay' and try to walk in a circle around him. Keep showing him the palm of your hand and say 'stay', particularly before you walk around the back of him.

♦ Now try asking your puppy to stay while there are distractions around. Practise in the park or where there are other temptations about.

You can make your stays harder and harder, and as time goes by you can progress to moving out of sight.

COMMON PROBLEMS AND SOLUTIONS TO THE 'STAY'

My puppy always sits but jumps straight up again – I don't even get the opportunity to tell him to stay

This means that you need to get a better sit or down before you try the stay. Use a treat to ask your puppy to sit, as detailed in the earlier chapter. When your puppy sits you should hold onto the treat for a few seconds before feeding it to your puppy. Often, owners feed their treat immediately when their puppy sits. Most puppies will then get straight up because they have received their reward. If your puppy gets straight up as you feed the treat, remove it and tell him to sit again. By holding onto the treat for a few seconds, you will teach your puppy to remain in that position, and it is when you are at this point you can begin to practise the stay. Be patient, calm and persevere, you will get there.

My puppy will stay when in front of me but when I walk away he always gets up to follow me

You probably need to get a more reliable stay before moving away. You may also need to increase your reward for when your puppy does stay. Remember to aim for 15 to 20 seconds before you even attempt moving away. Each time you practise, reward your puppy with a treat when his stay is completed, this will help reinforce that he is doing the right thing by keeping in the 'stay'. Don't forget that when you begin to walk away, walk slowly, one step at a time and don't turn your back on him at this stage.

When I walk back towards to my puppy, he gets up to come and meet me

♦ This is normally because a puppy has been rewarded for doing so. You need to be good with your timing in order to clearly communicate to your puppy what you are looking for. Are you rewarding your puppy at the wrong time? I often see owners reward their puppy when they return, even though their dog has got up to greet them. Don't forget that a reward is not only a treat, but stroking, touching or eye contact will also be taken as praise.

♦ If your puppy has started getting up to come and meet you, calmly take him back to the place he started in, put him back into a 'stay' and then start again. Also, you may need to practise easier stays – remember to get success before you move on to harder exercises.

♦ Have you been calling your puppy to you at the end of the stay? Remember you should always return to your puppy to finish the stay exercise. Never call him up out of a stay.

When I return to my puppy, he gets up just as I get back to him

♦ Most likely a case of being rewarded too early. You should always reward your puppy while they are in the stay, in the actual position in which you left them. If your puppy gets up when you return, simply put him back in the position and reward him there.

♦ You should also remind him that you want him to stay, so as you approach him on your return – show him the palm of your hand and say 'stay'.

We have done the basics but when I try to leave the room with my puppy in a stay he keeps getting up

You may be trying to accomplish this exercise too early. For a puppy, learning the stay can be quite a hard exercise, it requires a lot of concentration and self-control. We all know how much puppies love to run around and play and here you are asking them not to. You must have achieved a really good stay with your puppy before you even attempt to go out of his sight. He should be capable of remaining in a stay even when things are going on around him. If you have reached this level of training already – then remember to build up to leaving the room slowly. When you first practise, do so for only a second and then return. Use the same principles as when you began training, start slowly and gradually make it more difficult by leaving for longer periods.

10

Playtime and Tricks

This chapter is to give you a few ideas for games and tricks you can teach your puppy. The list of activities you can enjoy with your dog is endless, but in these early days you should find the few listed here quite good fun. Remember that it is meant to be fun, and if your puppy doesn't get it straight away, keep practising in short sessions and he should get there eventually.

> For training purposes, remember your puppy will learn well if whatever you are doing is fun, so you should break up the serious stuff with some of these activities – incorporating tricks and games into your training makes it fun, enjoyable and different for you both.

Learning tricks is great stimulation for any dog and practising them are a great way for you to better understand your puppy's thought process. You will see how dogs learn by association, and it will improve your timing as you practise rewarding at exactly the right time in order to communicate your message successfully.

With all of these tricks, by using a treat to lure your puppy you are automatically putting a hand signal to the action. When you are ready to try asking your puppy to perform a trick without you luring, remember to use the hand signal he will have been learning. For example, when you say 'roll over', do the circle movement with your hand.

GIVE A PAW

1. Start by asking your puppy to sit.

2. Gently lift up a paw.

3. As you lift his paw, say 'paw' and feed a treat.

4. Release the paw.

5. After a few days try holding out your hand and say 'paw' – your puppy should understand what you mean – if not, keep practising, he probably just needs a little longer.

ROLL-OVER

1. Start by asking your puppy to 'down'. He needs to be lying down with his weight over onto one side.

2. Hold a treat right in front of your puppy's nose. Slowly move the treat so his head twists round towards his shoulder and he starts rolling over onto his back.

3. As he rolls over onto his back, keep pulling the treat round so that you lure him all the way over onto his other side. You can say 'over' as he is doing this.

4. Stand up, clap your hands and say 'up'. As your puppy jumps up, feed him the treat.

TWIST

1. Start with your puppy at your left-hand side in a walking position.

2. Keeping a treat in your left hand, hold it right in front of your puppy's nose. Keep the treat level with his nose, be careful you don't lift it up too high.

3. Lure your puppy to twist, making a large circle with your arm. Move your arm away from you, so your puppy turns away from you and not in towards you.

4. As your puppy is twisting, say the word 'twist'.

5. When he has mastered the twist, you can practise twisting him the opposite way, using the direction of your arm to signal which way you want him to turn.

CATCH

1. Start with your puppy in a sit.

2. Show your puppy the treat you are holding.

3. Say 'catch' and throw the treat towards your puppy. Don't stand too far away or throw the treat too high to start with.

4. After a few practises, your puppy will learn that 'catch' precedes a treat coming and he will then attempt to catch it.

BACK-UP

1. Start with your puppy in front of you.

2. Hold a treat and place it right in front of your puppy's nose.

3. Start to walk towards your puppy so he has to walk backwards to get out of your way.

4. As he takes a couple of steps backwards, say 'back' and finish by feeding him the treat.

5. As he gets better, gradually increase the steps you take and eventually, stop walking yourself.

> **TIP**
>
> This is a useful trick to apply to your everyday life. For example, when you come into the room and your puppy is blocking your path. As pack leader you should expect him to move out of your way. Teaching this trick will help give you a command to ensure this will happen.

HIDE AND SEEK

This game of hide and seek involves using your puppy's toys. You can teach your puppy the names of his different toys and send him out to find them. Start by throwing a toy for him and encouraging him to bring the toy back to you. When he does so, praise him by saying 'Good Boy' – followed by the name of the toy. You can also treat him as he brings the toy back to you.

Practise naming just one or two toys to begin with, making sure that your timing is perfect: that is, putting the name to the toy when your puppy is holding it or looking directly at it. You can also hold the toy and say its name. When you throw it, say 'Fetch the _____'. As long as you use your word at the right time, plenty of times, he will associate that toy with the name you have given it.

When you think he understands the name of the toy, throw out a couple of toys and send him to collect the one you ask for. If he gets it right, praise him and offer a reward. If he gets it wrong, say nothing and do not offer a reward. Throw the toys back and try again. If he consistently gets it wrong – you need to go back a step and practise naming the toy as he probably hasn't understood properly yet.

When your puppy knows the name of a few toys, you can try hiding them in the garden or around the house and sending him to find the one you ask for. I have met some owners who play this game with members of their household. They use the same principle in teaching their names, and then all run and hide while someone remains behind to tell him who to go and find. Remember to reward him well when he finds the correct person and he will soon learn all of your family's names.

FOOD HUNT

This is a very simple game which is great for occupying your puppy and providing mental stimulation. You can do it indoors, although I prefer the garden due to the extra space and variety of places to hide the food.

Use dried food from your puppy's daily allowance. A good idea is to use the food hunt to feed one of his meals, perhaps the morning one.

Start by showing him the food and throw it a little way from you. When he has gone to eat it, start again with another piece and gradually increase the distance that you throw the food away from you.

When your puppy has the idea that you are spreading the food around for him to find, you can hide it all around the garden, under bushes and plastic plant pots. In fact anywhere that he can go and hunt it out!

To keep him guessing, you could add a few different treats into the hunt which will keep him interested and ensure he enjoys the hunt all the more.

The food hunt is quick and easy to set up and many dogs really enjoy it, particularly those who are food motivated or enjoy sniffing and working such as Spaniels. Even dogs who are not especially motivated by food can enjoy this game: you may find that the challenge of hunting and working for food as he would in the wild, will make him more interested than just being it offered it up in a bowl.

Index